ADVANCE PRAISE FOR *THE SECRETS OF COLLEGE SUCCESS*

"If I had my way, I'd give this book to every single college student, of any age, and *make* them read it. A book that moves from 'How to Turn a B into an A' to '10 Surefire Ways to Piss Off Your Professor,' is beyond just 'helpful.'' It is 'the Missing Manual' for turning a merely 'okay' college experience into a delicious adventure. I laughed, I took notes, I loved every page. And I'm not even in college. If you are, don't even think about not buying this book. It will be the best thing you ever did for yourself."

—*Richard Bolles, author of* What Color Is Your Parachute?

"Along with shower flip-flops and a very loud alarm clock, this book should be on every freshman's college packing list. The professors have outlined solutions for all the major fears that students face when they start college."

—*Marjorie Savage, parent program director, University of Minnesota and author of* You're on Your Own (But I'm Here If You Need Me): Mentoring Your Child During the College Years

"Psychologically sound tips for thriving, not just surviving, in college. Lynn's and Jeremy's tips will make your college experience a spectacular success."

—*Chuck Snowden, director of honors program, University of Wisconsin*

"Clear, practical, comprehensive — and caring. These authors want you to succeed. Listen."

—*Judy Genshaft, president, University of South Florida and past president, American Council on Education*

"Riddled with humor and witty in presentation, this lighthearted 'easy read' could be the most helpful, honest resource for today's college student."

—*Scott H. Reikofski, director, fraternity/sorority affairs, University of Pennsylvania*

"*The Secrets of College Success* needs to be required reading for anyone starting college, regardless of age. A great source of practical advice that could mean the difference between success and failure."

—*Eduardo J. Padrón, president, Miami Dade College*

"The students who are most successful in college are those who are most prepared. *The Secrets of College Success* reveals what students need to know from the perspective of the professors who teach them. It pays to know the rules of the game before you play."

—*George R. Boggs, president and CEO, American Association of Community Colleges*

"This volume provides a banquet of tips. Easy to read, easy to locate what you need, this book will be helpful throughout your undergraduate years. I highly recommend it."

—*Sharon J. Hamilton, professor and former director, Indiana University Faculty Colloquium on Excellence in Teaching*

"Accessibly written and logically organized, there's something here for everyone. This handy volume will help students focus on what it takes to be successful."

—*Peter H. Quimby, deputy dean, Princeton University*

"This book provides sound advice in a great format on how to get the most from your college education, starting on Day 1 of your freshman year."

—*Martha O'Connell, executive director, Colleges that Change Lives*

"High schools focus on getting their seniors TO college but they rarely teach them how to get THROUGH college. Professors Jacobs and Hyman fill this gap with a series of high energy, digestible and practical tips that any student can master in one sitting. This book should be required reading for every college-bound student so that they will be equipped with the 'under-the-hood' expertise they need to succeed in higher education."

—*Keith W. Frome, chief academic officer, College Summit Inc.*

"*The Secrets of College Success* is an easy-to-read, highly informative book. In my experience, many students come in to Stanford unprepared for the realities of college life. With bite-sized and digestible tips, this book provides substantial advice applicable to any college student."

—*Kamil Dada, president and editor in chief, The Stanford Daily, Stanford University*

Professors' Guide™

THE SECRETS OF
COLLEGE SUCCESS

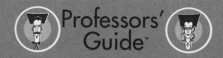

Professors'
Guide™

THE SECRETS OF
COLLEGE SUCCESS

Lynn F. Jacobs and Jeremy S. Hyman

JB JOSSEY-BASS
A Wiley Imprint
www.josseybass.com

Published by Jossey-Bass

A Wiley Imprint

989 Market Street, San Francisco, CA 94103-1741—www.josseybass.com

Readers should be aware that Internet Web sites offered as citations and/or sources for fur-ther information may have changed or disappeared between the time this was written and when it is read.

Jossey-Bass books and products are available through most bookstores. To contact Jossey-Bass directly call our Customer Care Department within the U.S. at 800-956-7739, outside the U.S. at 317-572-3986, or fax 317-572-4002.

Jossey-Bass also publishes its books in a variety of electronic formats. Some content that appears in print may not be available in electronic books.

Library of Congress Cataloging-in-Publication Data

Jacobs, Lynn F.
  The secrets of college success / Lynn F. Jacobs and Jeremy S. Hyman.
      p. cm.—(Professors' guide ; 1)
  Includes index.
  ISBN 978-0-470-87466-0 (pbk.)
  1. College student orientation—United States. 2. College students—United States—Conduct of life. 3. College students—Time management—United States. I. Hyman, Jeremy S. II. Title.
  LB2343.32J35 2010
  378.1'98—dc22

                                      2010019247

Printed in the United States of America.

FIRST EDITION

PB Printing 10 9 8 7 6 5 4 3 2 1

MEET THE PROFESSORS

Dr. Lynn F. Jacobs is professor of art history at the University of Arkansas. A specialist in northern Renaissance art, Lynn previously taught at Vanderbilt University, California State University, Northridge, the University of Redlands, and NYU. She has received the National Endowment for the Humanities Fellowship twice and the University of Arkansas Prize for distinguished academic advising.

Jeremy S. Hyman is founder and chief architect of *Professors' Guide*™ content projects. An expert in early modern philosophy, Jeremy has taught at the University of Arkansas, UCLA, MIT, and Princeton University. He received the University of California Regents' award for distinguished teaching.

Lynn and Jeremy are co-authors of the book *Professors' Guide to Getting Good Grades in College* (HarperCollins, 2006). They write a weekly column at *U.S. News & World Report*, WWW.USNEWS.COM/PROFESSORSGUIDE, and they blog at *Reader's Digest, Huffington Post*, and *Fastweb.com*.

Lynn and Jeremy live in Fayetteville, Arkansas, with their son, Jonah. Their Web site is WWW.PROFESSORSGUIDE.COM and you can reach them at PROFESSORS@PROFESSORSGUIDE.COM. We'd love to hear from you. No kidding.

CONTENTS

8   THE SECOND HALF OF COLLEGE

9   THE END—AND THE BEGINNING

INTRODUCTION

You might not know this, but you're going to college at the very best time in the last five hundred years. New media, twenty-first-century technologies, better professors, government funding for college—all of these go together to make this a wonderful time to be at college.

That is—if you know what to do.

You might have thought professors and advisers would tell you all you need to know. You wouldn't be right. Some professors think part of college is figuring out on your own what's expected. Others think it's a waste of class time to go over how to manage your time, study, prepare for tests, or write papers. Still others think that if they tell you what to do, you'll think it's a recipe for an A, which, if you don't get, will result in a colossal grade dispute—something no professor wants.

And, at some colleges, the booming enrollments have simply made it impossible for professors, advisers, and staff to give you the advice and attention you need and deserve—no matter how much they'd like to.

And so we've written *The Secrets of College Success*—the first book to offer quick tips, all written by professors, that'll help you achieve your full potential at college. Whether you're a beginning or advanced student; whether you're at a four-year college, community college, or taking courses on the Web; whether you're already doing pretty well at college or maybe not as well as you'd like; even if you're a high school student just beginning to think about college—this book is for you.

The secrets we reveal and the tips that we offer are the product of over thirty years of teaching experience at eight different colleges—big and small, private colleges and state universities, good schools and not-all-that-good schools. Over ten thousand students have tried the tips—and we can tell you they really work.

Most of all, this book is fun to read. You'll find yourself not only strategizing about college—figuring our how you can apply our tips to your own college experience—but making up tips of your own and even wanting to share them with others. And you'll enjoy your success when you find that the tips—both yours and ours—have changed the way you approach college.

Congratulations. This is a wonderful time to be at college. Make the most of it.

Lynn and Jeremy

Top 10 Reasons to Read This Book

#10. **The tips are really good**. Written wholly by professors, the tips in this book give you high-value information about what to do at college—and what *not* to do.

#9. **The information is not available elsewhere**. No professor, adviser, or college guide will tell you the insider secrets we reveal in this book.

#8. **The information is quick.** *Top 10 Lists, Do's and Don'ts, To-Do Lists, How-to Guides*—all the advice is bite-sized and easy to digest. And our *Professors' Guide*™ icons will help you navigate your way through the book.

#7. **The tips are practical.** No abstract theories here, just concrete, easy-to-follow tips that you can use to guarantee your success at college.

#6. **We tell you everything you need to know—and *only* the things you need to know.** From the summer before college to the crucial first year of college, from picking a major to finding a job—all the key moments of college are covered.

#5. **The tips are up-to-date**. Electronic resources, first-year experience courses, Facebook and Skype, e-readers and online courses, double and triple majors, closed courses, research on the Web, internships and study abroad—all the new realities of college are included. And we give you links to useful Web sites, so you can find out the latest information about special topics.

#4. **Each tip stands on its own**. You can use as many—or as few—of the tips as you want and still get excellent results. And you can follow the tips in any order. Pick a tip that interests you and then move on to others, or just randomly flip to a page and start reading.

#3.   **We tell you what to do**. Like a good undergraduate adviser (something sorely lacking at many colleges), we tell you not just what you *might* do, but what you *should* do. In a friendly and supportive voice, of course.

#2.   **The tips are time-tested**. The advice in this book has worked for over ten thousand students. And it will work for you.

And the number-one reason you should read this book:

#1.   **The tips are fun to read**. You'll enjoy thinking about different strategies for college success as you read through our tips. And, in the best case, you'll LOL as you read some of our attempts at humor. (At least you won't be bored.)

The Professors' Guide™ Icons

Here are the icons used in this book—and what they mean:

 EXTRA POINTER. An additional tip that fills out another tip or applies to a special situation.

 5-STAR TIP. A really high-value suggestion that you should be sure to use. One of the best tips in the book.

 BEST-KEPT SECRET. One of the things that no one wants you to know, but that will help you do really well at college.

 REALITY CHECK. An invitation to take a step back and assess what's really going on.

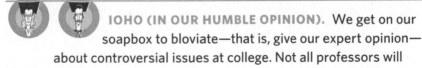 **IOHO (IN OUR HUMBLE OPINION).** We get on our soapbox to bloviate—that is, give our expert opinion—about controversial issues at college. Not all professors will agree.

 BONUS TIP. For those who can't get enough, one more tip.

FLASH! Late-breaking information worth knowing about.

Except where Web sites are very familiar (such as Google, Amazon, BN, or eBay), we've given the entire Web address, for example, WWW.OCW.MIT.EDU. Some URLs, for who knows what reason, omit the "WWW." We've written these as, for example, HTTP://OCW.ND.EDU.

Professors' Guide™

THE SECRETS OF
COLLEGE SUCCESS

1

THIS IS COLLEGE

Going to college is a very special sort of experience. It's a time of tremendous personal growth. A time when some students get their first serious taste of independence, while others find their BFFLs, increase their Facebook friends exponentially, or even meet up with their future spouses. But even more important, college is also a time of great intellectual growth. A chance to study things you didn't even know existed or to delve into topics you do know about at a level of detail and sophistication that you've never before imagined.

Because college is so special, it's important to make the most of it. To squeeze all the juice out of it and drink it all up. Especially when it comes to the academic side of things, where students often don't reap all the benefits college has to offer. This chapter will help you understand what college is all about—to get a real picture of what you are about to go through or are already going through. And it will offer basic tips about the things that matter most at college.

In this chapter you'll learn:

▶ 10 Things You Need to Know About College (but Probably Don't)

▶ What's New at College? Fun Facts

▶ The 14 Habits of Top College Students

▶ The 11 Secrets of Getting Good Grades in College

▶ 6 Things You Didn't Know About Grading (but Really Should)

▶ 12 Ways to Get Your Money's Worth out of College

▶ The College Student's Bill of Rights

10 Things You Need to Know About College (but Probably Don't)

1. **You're in charge of this thing.** For many students, the most striking thing about college is that there's no one there to hold your hand. Picking courses, getting to class, doing the reading, and figuring out what's going to be on the test and what's expected on the papers— all of these are things you're going to have to do pretty much on your own. Sure, there are profs (and, in some schools, TAs) who'll give instructions and offer suggestions from time to time. But you're the one who'll have to take responsibility for hauling your butt out of bed when it's ten degrees below zero—or one hundred and five, depending on what school you're at—and doing what you need to do.

2. **Your parents may not be much help.** Some students are on their iPhone five times a day looking for advice from Mom or Dad. But even the best-intentioned parents can lead you astray. Colleges are different—and, in many cases, much improved—from what they were twenty-five years ago, and professors' expectations have changed accordingly. Suggestion: tune down (or, in some cases, tune out) the parents until you have a firm handle on what's expected at your college—today.

3. **Attendance isn't required—but is expected.** One of the first things many students discover is that college classes can be huge: 100, 200, and, at some state schools, even 700 students in a lecture. In such an anonymous environment, it's the easiest thing in the world to tell yourself there's no good reason to bother going to class. (Even if your school has small classes, attendance typically counts for only a tiny percentage of the grade, if at all.) But professors assume you've made all the classes, and they have no hesitation about asking a midterm or final question that focuses on the contents of a single lecture. Kinda makes you want to go, doesn't it?

4. **Content is doled out in large units.** You may be used to getting your content in short, entertaining blasts: the one- to three-minute YouTube video, the abbreviation-filled IM, the 140-character tweet. But the professor is thinking in terms of the fifty-minute lecture, divided into only two or three main segments; and the author of the journal article is thinking in terms of twenty-five pages of densely written argument, divided into perhaps three or four main sections. Bottom line? You've got to adjust your focus from quick bursts of content to sustained argument. And retrain your attention span to process long—very long, it'll seem—units of content.

5. **Up to two-thirds of the work is done outside of class.** Contrary to what you might have heard, the lecture portion of the course is the least time-consuming activity. That's because (with the exception of a few very basic, introductory courses) the professor is expecting the bulk of the work to be done by you, on your own. Doing the reading and homework; preparing for the quizzes, tests, and presentations; doing research and writing papers—all of these are activities that can easily eat up more than half the time you put into any given course.

6. **A C is a really bad grade.** Many first-year college students—and even some students who've been at college for a while—think that if they get C's in all their classes they're doing just fine—or, at least, adequately. But what these folks need to know is that in some college courses the grade distribution is 20 to 30 percent A's, 30 to 60 percent B's, and only 15 to 30 percent C's. Set your sights accordingly.

7. **Not everyone who teaches is a prof.** At many state universities—especially those where the student-faculty ratio is 15 to 1 or greater—much of the teaching is done by graduate students. At some of the better state schools (the University of California and the University of Texas, for instance), only very advanced graduate students are allowed to teach their own courses. But at other schools (we won't mention names because we want to keep our jobs), the lecturer can be a first-year graduate student, who might not even have majored in the field in college. Moral? Whenever possible, take courses with regular faculty, who'll be more experienced and, in the best cases, will actually have done research in the subject they're teaching.

BEST-KEPT SECRET. Colleges don't always list the name of the instructor in the course description or at the online registration site. Sometimes it's because they've made last-minute appointments, hiring some adjunct or TA a few weeks before the semester starts. But sometimes it's because they don't want to highlight how few of the courses are taught by the regular faculty. Go to the department office the week before classes start and ask who's scheduled to teach the courses you're interested in— and what his or her status is.

IOHO. Graduate students at universities are often compared to residents at teaching hospitals. But the analogy is misleading. Residents are full-fledged doctors who have completed their medical degrees; graduate students are not professors and have not completed their terminal degrees (in most fields, the PhD).

8. **It's the product that counts.** Many students think that *effort* counts. That's why, when papers are returned, there's always a line of students waiting to argue how many hours they worked, how many articles they read, and how hard they've been trying in the course. The thing is, in college what counts most is the *product*: the paper (not how it was produced), the test (not how much you studied for it), and the oral presentation (not how much you knew about the subject, but couldn't quite get out).

9. **Understanding is more than just memorizing.** While some intro courses require some memorizing (vocabulary in foreign languages, theorems in math, names and dates in history), other beginning courses will include essays on the exams. And in virtually every advanced or upper-division course, you'll be asked not just to regurgitate what you've memorized from the lecture or textbook, but to do some analysis, apply the concepts to some new cases, or organize the material or data in some new or interesting way. Pretty different from what you might be used to.

10. **The prof's on your side—and *wants* to help.** Many students see the professor as an enemy to be defeated—the person who'll trick you with all sorts of gotcha questions on the test and who's very stingy come grade time. But really the professor is eager to teach you and (believe it or not) would like to see you do well. That's because, in many cases, he or she has forgone a much more lucrative career in business or industry for the sole purpose of educating college students—like yourself. So when the prof invites you to come to an office hour, go to a review session, or just communicate by e-mail, Skype, or Facebook, consider the possibility that the professor really means it. Because he or she probably does.

What's New at College? Fun Facts

✔ There are almost 20 million students enrolled in U.S. colleges—a number growing at 4.5 percent a year.

✔ Almost 60 percent of college students are women, and 40 percent of college students are over the age of twenty-five.

✔ Community colleges are booming: over one-third of college students go to one.

✔ The *average* list price for tuition at a private college is $27,000, at a state university $7,000 (for those who live in that state), and at a community college $2,500—*a year.* (At some schools, the prices are considerably higher.)

✔ College tuition went up by an average of 6 percent last year—and every other year for the last ten.

✔ About 75 percent of full-time college students receive financial aid. And there are numerous tax benefits for all students.

✔ A recent study pegged the lifetime increased earnings potential of someone with a college degree at $279,893 (not a million dollars, as previously thought).

✔ Over 90 percent of college students are on Facebook (MySpace, Hi5, and Friendster are considered uncool). The average college student spends about half an hour a day on social networking.

✔ Only about 10 percent of college students belong to a fraternity or sorority.

✔ Four of the eight Ivy League presidents are women.

✔ Many colleges have new first-year experience courses or freshman seminars to help students find their place in the college community.

✔ Many students today fulfill their language requirement with Mandarin Chinese, Arabic, or Japanese—not Spanish, French, or German.

✔ The most popular majors are business, psychology, nursing, history and social sciences, biology, education, and communications. (Classics, astronomy, film studies, aviation, and chemical engineering have the fewest takers.)

✔ The most lucrative majors are petroleum engineering and civil engineering. (The job prospects aren't so good in English, classics, philosophy, and art history.)

✔ E-textbooks and e-resources are rapidly replacing print books and brick-and-mortar libraries. Many students read their textbooks on e-readers, and some students even rent their books.

✔ "Smart" classrooms allow professors to incorporate PowerPoint presentations, videos, and other content into their lectures. Some professors use "clickers" that allow students to offer instant input on how well they've understood the lecture.

✔ Some college courses are conducted online, either at the university's own Web site, through iTunesU, the OpenCourseWare initiative, or Academic Earth. (Some students wonder why they should go to class at all.)

✔ Many colleges offer service learning programs: you get college credit for volunteering to do community service.

✔ Some schools require a year of study abroad: globalization comes to college.

✔ The graduation rate at U.S. colleges is only slightly more than 50 percent—something we hope to change with this book.

The 14 Habits of Top College Students

What makes some college students successful while others—well, less so? Sometimes it's a question of intelligence or insight. And sometimes it's sheer good luck. But a lot of the time it's a question of good habits: things you do on a regular basis that set you aside from the hordes of other, more scattered, students. In the hopes of separating the sheep from the goats, we present the following fourteen habits of top-notch college students. You'll find that these folk:

1. **Have a schedule.** Not only do they know when the tests and papers fall in the semester, but they have a good sense of what work needs to be done each week as the semester progresses. Nice and balanced: everything in gear and no worries come exam time.

2. **Divide up the tasks.** Readings get broken up into manageable chunks (not two hundred pages in one sitting). Quizzes and tests are studied for over the course of a week (not at 3 a.m. the night before). And paper ideas start gestating when the assignment is handed out (not the day before it's due, when you can barely formulate an idea, much less think through an issue).

3. **Are organized.** It's impossible to do any real work when you don't have the tools for the job: a working computer with the right software, a fast Internet connection, a good printer, and, for some courses, a thorough knowledge of how to navigate the course Web page and the university and library portals. Not to mention the basic materials of the course: a full set of lecture notes, the textbooks and articles, and, of course, all the course handouts and assignments.

4. **Hang out with smart friends.** Successful students know that spending lots of time with friends who don't even know what courses they're taking—or why they're in college at all—can create an atmosphere so toxic that any attempts to do well immediately wither and die. Pick your cohorts as carefully as you pick your courses.

5. **Don't kid themselves.** For instance, when you think you're study-ing, but you're really tweeting about how you barely survived your bonfire-jumping last night. Or when you're alternating between read-ing the e-article and checking out your friend's Facebook page every eight seconds or so. You're the easiest person you know to deceive. Don't.

6. **Manage their feelings.** It's difficult to excel in a course if you're feeling inadequate, bummed out, or doomed to fail. Students who know how to focus on their own positive achievements—rather than on what they got on the quiz that counts for about 2 percent of the course grade—have a leg up on the rest.

7. **Challenge themselves.** Good students are intellectually ener-getic. When they read, they think actively about what they're read-ing. When they go to class, they don't just veg out or text. On tests, they pounce on the questions and answer them directly and fully (this distinguishes their work from their colleagues trying to BS their way through the question). And on papers they look for deeper levels of meaning and more nuanced points—always a hit with the professor.

8. **Are consistent—and persistent.**

   Tired or hung over? "I'm still going to make it to that 9 a.m. lecture."

   Late-night review session? "Like the owl, I do my best work at night."

   Difficult problem set? "I'll get these right if it kills me."

   Three-hour final? "I'll stay to the bitter end. Maybe I can touch up my essay and collect a few extra points."

9. **Are open to feedback.** While it's easy and more fun to toss away your graded papers and exams, or conveniently forget to pick them up, the best students carefully study the comments and go over any mistakes they've made. And when the next piece of work rolls around, they take another look at the previous set of comments to see if there are any mistakes that they can correct on the new piece of work. All without feeling wounded or defensive.

10. **Ask when they don't understand.** Look, you've got a mouth. So when you don't get something in the reading, in the lecture, or in the homework, ask someone who might know. Like the prof or TA, for example.

11. **Aren't too shy.** Sure, everyone feels intimidated about having to seek out the professor (or even the TA) to talk about their own work. But keep in mind that most professors *enjoy* talking with students and, if asked, will offer loads of help on papers, preparing for tests, and even finding topics for future work—say, a junior project, senior thesis, or internship or collaboration. (See "The 15 Secrets of Going to See the Professor" on pp. 129–133 for our very best tips on how to approach the Man [or Woman].)

12. **Look out for Number One.** While some students are willing to blow off a week of school to satisfy the needs of others—for example, a demanding boss during busy season or an Uncle Fred who schedules his third wedding two days before finals—good students know that college is their job and make doing well their highest priority. Especially during the college busy season—the last month of the semester, when those big-ticket items like the term paper and the final exam roll around, and two-thirds of the grade is won or lost.

13. **Keep themselves in tip-top shape.** It's difficult to do well if you're sick as a dog, haven't slept in a week, or are loaded up on some substance. Successful students manage their physical and emotional needs as carefully as they do their academic needs.

14. **Have a goal—and a plan.** The best students know why they're in college and what they need to do to achieve their goals. You can't do well if you don't know what you're doing—and why.

The 11 Secrets of Getting Good Grades in College

Grades are the measure of college success. Like the salary at a job, a batting average in baseball, or the price of a stock, your GPA is an objective indicator of how you're doing. And yet, there's surprisingly little good information—least of all from professors—about just what you should do to get good grades. We go where others fear to tread. And so, here are the eleven secrets of getting really good grades in college (A's, we mean):

1. **Take control of your destiny.** Your grade destiny, that is. There's no teacher or parent to remind you every day what you need to do, or to make sure you've studied for exams. It's all in your hands. So step up to the plate and take responsibility. The grades you get will depend on what you yourself do.

2. **Don't overload.** Some students think it's a mark of pride to take as many course hours as the college allows. It isn't. Take four or, at the most, five courses each semester. That way you'll be able to devote all your energies to a manageable number of subjects, and you won't have to sacrifice quality for quantity. (For our best tips on which courses to take, see "Do's and Don'ts for Picking Your Courses" on pp. 34–36.)

3. **Get your a** to class.** Most students have a cutting budget: the number of lectures they think they can miss in each course and still do well. But if there are thirty-five class meetings, each class contains 3 percent of the content: miss seven classes, and you've missed 20 percent of the material.

BEST-KEPT SECRET. Some not-so-nice professors want to penalize students who blow off the class right before Thanksgiving or Spring Break. So they pick an essay question for the final exam from that very lecture. End result? You can do really major damage to your GPA for the price of just one class.

4. **Take really good notes.** In many intro courses, the professor's lectures form the major part of the material tested on the midterm and final. So as you're taking notes, you're really writing the textbook for the course—which in many cases is more important than the official textbook. Be sure to get down everything the professor says and to maintain your notes in an organized and readable form. After all, these are the notes you'll have to study a number of times later in the course. (For primo note-taking tips, see "10 Secrets of Taking Excellent Lecture Notes," pp. 59–62.)

5. **Study like you mean it.** There's a difference between studying and "studying"—and you know what it is. When you're really studying, you're 100 percent focused on and engaged with the material: a total immersion in what you're doing and a strong desire to get it right. When you're only half-heartedly studying, you're really only 35 percent involved, with the other 65 percent of your attention divided among tweeting your friend about how much you're studying, scoping out the surrounding tables to see who else might be around (and how attractive they are), and daydreaming about all the fun things you'll do when you finish this awful studying. Look, we know studying can be painful, but all students who get A's do it—no matter what they tell you. (For our best study tips, see the "How-*Not*-to-Study Guide" on pp. 55–58.)

6. **Do all the homework.** You might think the homework and problem sets—each of which is worth maybe 0.1 percent of the grade—are just busywork: something the professor assigns to make sure you're doing something in the course each week. But really, the homework provides applications of the concepts, principles, and methods of the field to actual examples—the same sort of examples that will come up on the bigger tests. If you do well on the homework—that is, get ten out of ten on the problem sets or a check-plus on the little writing exercises—you're putting yourself in a good position to get a 100 when it really counts—on the midterm or final.

7. **Take each test three times.** When done right, taking a test is really three activities: preparing for the test, taking the actual exam, then going over the comments to see what mistakes you made. Each activity furnishes important—and grade-improving—information: the

studying gives you practice in questions very similar to the those that will be on the test; the actual test is where the A is earned (at least in the best case); and the review of the comments (often accompanied by a visit to the professor's office hour to clear up anything unclear) is an investment in an A on the next test. (For our best advice about tests, see "12 Tips for A+ Test Preparation" on pp. 100–104, "So What's Going to Be on the Test Anyway?" on pp. 105–107, and "Top 13 Test-Taking Tips" on pp. 108–112.)

8. **Always answer the question asked.** More points are lost on tests and papers by not answering the question asked than by giving the wrong answer. That's because students often have strong—and wrong—preconceptions about what the professor should be asking. "How can the question be so specific?" they wonder. "How can the professor not be asking a question about last week's classes, especially since he (or she) seemed so interested in that topic?" "Can the professor *really* be asking about that journal article we were supposed to read, or about the discussion in section?" Don't try to psych out the professor or distrust what you see before your very eyes. Answer the question, as asked, head-on. (If you're not sure what's meant, always ask—and rescue your grade.)

9. **Play all four quarters.** Many college courses are "back-loaded." More than half the grade is left to assignments due the last month of the semester: a third test, 15 percent; the term (or research) paper, 25 percent; the cumulative final, 30 percent. You get the idea. Pace yourself and don't run out of gas just as you're coming into the home stretch.

10. **Do all the "extras."** In some courses, there are special end-of-the-semester activities that can improve your grade. Review sessions, extra office hours, rewrites of papers, extra-credit work—all of these can be grade-boosters. Especially in schools where there are no pluses and minuses, even a few extra points can push your borderline grade over the hump (from, say, a B-plus to an A-minus—that is, an A).

11. **Join a community.** Many students improve their grades by working with study buddies or study groups. Try to meet at least once a

week—especially in courses in which there are weekly problem sets or quizzes. And if your school offers "freshman clusters" in which a group of students all take the same section of some required courses, sign up for them, too. Students can improve their grades one level or more when they commit to working in an organized way with other students.

 5-STAR TIP.   Resolve to get at least one A each semester. Getting even a single A will change the way you think about yourself: you'll be more confident about your abilities and more energized for future semesters. If you're at all close in even one course, work really hard to do it. It will change things forever.

6 Things You Didn't Know About Grading (but Really Should)

Given how concerned most students are about grades, it's amazing how little they know about how grading is done. Or maybe it's not so amazing. Universities go to great lengths to hide—or, at least, not to disclose—facts about grading that anyone who's taught at a university for more than a year is fully aware of. After all, knowledge is power, and no university wants students to have that much power. Luckily for you, we have the six secrets of grading that no one wants you to know. Intrigued? Take a peek.

1. **It's ten minutes—then on to the next.** You might think that your grader will spend half an hour to an hour grading each student's piece of work. Not likely. Unfortunately, given that an instructor might have a stack of thirty, forty, or even seventy papers or tests to grade, he or she has only ten minutes to devote to each piece of work—fifteen minutes, tops. This is why you should get right to the point, make your claims clearly and forcefully, avoid any irrelevant or unnecessary material, and take the trouble to really explain your points. (For more on this, see "10 Tips for Writing the Perfect Paper" on pp. 113–116.)

2. **The grading is often outsourced.** In large classes at big colleges, the professor giving the lecture is rarely the person who does the grading. Instead there is usually a cadre of low-paid grad students who do the grading (at some schools, even advanced undergraduates can be graders). You might know the grad student as the TA running your discussion section, but your grader might also be an unseen and unnamed person who has been hired only to grade the written work. Some professors actively manage the grad student or grader, going over sample papers and setting a grading scale. But other professors are happy to delegate the whole job to the underling and never set eyes on student work (kind of amazing when you think about it).

3. **It's not as subjective as you think.** While it's pretty easy to see how grades are assigned on "objective" tests (like multiple-choice or short-answer tests), it's tempting to think that the grading of essays or papers is just a matter of opinion. But if you were to actually read a set of fifty essays on the same topic, you—and anyone who knew the material—could see right away that there is a wide range of levels of quality in the answers. For professors who have been teaching the material, it's extremely easy to sort the essays into those that show an excellent understanding of the issue, those that sorta get the point (but not really), and, finally, those that really have no idea what they're talking about. That's how A's, B's, and C's are created.

4. **A's are often in short supply.** Despite what you might have heard about grade inflation, it can be quite hard to get an A. At most colleges, professors give about 10 to 25 percent A's in introductory classes and perhaps 30 to 40 percent A's in more advanced courses (where students often are majors and further along in their college careers). (For tips on moving up to the A range, see "Top Ten Ways of Making the Leap from a B to an A" on p. 117.)

REALITY CHECK. You might have thought it's pretty easy to get good grades at college, given rampant grade inflation. But to see what the real story is, check out Professor Stuart Rojstaczer's WWW.GRADEINFLATION.COM. An interesting and comprehensive site very much recommended.

5. **Grading usually is not a zero-sum game.** In classes that are curved, your grade is in fact determined by your position relative to other students in the class. But curves are not used in all that many classes (liberal arts students don't see them all that often), and even when curves are used, professors sometimes make adjustments to achieve some absolute level for each of the major grade divisions. So relax—the reason you didn't get an A is not because your friend stole the last available A. It's because the level of your work didn't merit one.

6. **There's no real court of appeals.** Sure, most colleges have official procedures for disputing a grade, but grades actually get changed very, very rarely—and only if there is some serious procedural irregularity (such as the grader's incorrectly adding up the points, failing to read a page of the answer, or not following policies on the syllabus or college rules). Arguments that never work include "My friend wrote the same paper, but did better than I," "Another TA grades easier," and "The assignment wasn't fair." If you haven't gotten the grade you wanted, it's best just to suck it in, then ask the professor or TA how you can do better next time.

12 Ways to Get Your Money's Worth out of College

For some, it costs about as much as a Lexus ES. *Every year.* For others, about as much as a Honda Fit. And some will get change from a $5,000 bill. It's college, and, whatever way you slice it, it's very expensive. But cheer up. We've got a dozen tips to help you get your money's worth out of college. Even if you're laying out big bucks, at least you'll get more bang for your buck. Here's how:

1. **Take the choice courses, not the leftovers.** Always register for classes at the earliest possible date so you can select the courses you want, not get stuck with the dregs after every one else has registered. For first-year students, this means getting to the earliest orientation sessions, often held in (gasp!) June. But even later on, primo courses are available, provided you pick off-peak times. (For advice on how—and how not—to select classes, see "Do's and Don'ts for Picking Your Courses" on pp. 34–36 and "No Room at the Inn? What to Do When You're Closed Out of a Course" on pp. 37–38.)

2. **Get out of the herd.** Unlike the wildebeest, your safety is not in numbers. The best learning does not take place in large lecture courses, but in smaller classes, which can be found even at mega-universities—if you look carefully enough. Whenever you have a choice, size down. And when there's a choice of a professor or TA— well, wouldn't it be better to pick someone who has thought about the material for many years?

 5-STAR TIP. When given a choice between an online course and a regular lecture, you'll usually do better with the in-person course. The communication is generally better with a live lecturer, and, for most students, it's easier to concentrate in a classroom environment than lying in bed talking to your roommate.

3. **Make it to all your classes.** Some students think about their classes like fat cats with season tickets. They'll get to a few big games, but miss the snoozefests. But suppose we told you that you were paying by the class—say $100 or $200 a throw. Would you be so quick to cut? You do the math. You may be astonished at how much you've prepaid for each lecture—money that goes down the tube when you decide not to show.

4. **Use the facilities.** No, not *those* facilities. We're thinking about the recreational and academic services you paid for as part of your student fees: Olympic-size swimming pools, Apple-endowed computer labs—not to mention the free tutoring service, writing center, and math lab. And if you're not feeling up to par, or college isn't turning out to be quite as happy as you expected, be sure to check out the university health service or counseling center. You've already paid for them, too.

5. **Think about flying the coop.** At many schools, first-year students are required to live in the dorms. But after that, you're on your own. Consider living off-campus in an apartment or a cooperative living arrangement. You can often save bundles on food (at many colleges the food service is overpriced and is used to subsidize other campus programs). And hey, you might enjoy playing Rachael Ray, not to mention doing dishes once a month.

6. **Learn a skill for life.** Once you know your major, be on the lookout for courses that will give you the skills to get ahead in your chosen career (even if such courses are not required for the major). The ability to speak Chinese or Arabic could be a big selling point for a business major wanting to work for Walmart or Procter & Gamble—or the CIA or Homeland Security. A course in critical reasoning or logic could pay off for a wannabe lawyer—or a course in statistics for someone going into the health care profession. (For more on this, see "13 Skills You'll Need for a Career—and How to Get Them in College" on pp. 167–170.)

7. **Keep entering the lottery.** Many students (and parents) think that the financial aid package you get when you enter college is the end of the story. But once you're at college, there may be a number of

opportunities to compete for and get various hidden scholarships. Many donors give piles of money to specific departments for the support of their majors. Often these scholarships are handed out on the basis of merit, so if you're doing well, take full advantage of them.

8. **Hit up your uncle.** Uncle Sam, that is. To some degree, the pain of out-of-control tuition increases has been lessened by a slew of tax advantages including the American Opportunity Credit, the Hope Credit, and the Lifetime Learning Credit—as well as the Tuition and Fees Deduction and the Student Loan Interest Deduction. Be sure to educate yourself about all of these, then calculate your credit or deduction for each to see which one gives you the maximum benefit (many tax preparation software packages will do this for you automatically).

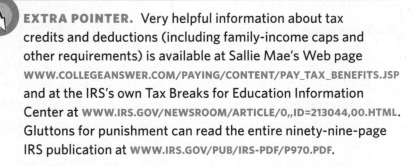

EXTRA POINTER. Very helpful information about tax credits and deductions (including family-income caps and other requirements) is available at Sallie Mae's Web page WWW.COLLEGEANSWER.COM/PAYING/CONTENT/PAY_TAX_BENEFITS.JSP and at the IRS's own Tax Breaks for Education Information Center at WWW.IRS.GOV/NEWSROOM/ARTICLE/0,,ID=213044,00.HTML. Gluttons for punishment can read the entire ninety-nine-page IRS publication at WWW.IRS.GOV/PUB/IRS-PDF/P970.PDF.

9. **Collaborate with a professor.** In many fields, there are real possibilities for work in tandem with a professor—coauthoring scholarly papers, presenting joint papers (or posters) at conferences, or interning. Many colleges are now putting big bucks into supporting these activities, which means you could end up with a stipend for research costs and travel. And, in the very best case, you'll join the professor's network of professional contacts, giving you a big leg up come looking-for-jobs time. Sweet.

10. **Travel on their dime.** Want to see the world? Consider the study abroad program. Many colleges have special scholarships or stipends

to enable students to do research abroad or to take courses at "sister" universities. This can be a wonderful opportunity to improve your language skills, to do research in countries where you can study the objects first-hand, and to take courses at colleges where they specialize in what you're interested in. (See "Top 10 Myths About Study Abroad" on pp. 171–174 for some tips.)

 5-STAR TIP. Make sure you have a valid *academic* reason for studying abroad. Hoping to find an Estonian bride or a Parisian groom won't cut the mustard at most colleges.

11. **Join the workforce.** At many colleges there are special work-study jobs to be had. Some of these—like being a museum guard or the checkout person at the college library—have long periods of downtime when you can catch up on your homework at the college's expense. And you'll make friends with other student-workers, not to mention getting in good with your parents (who'll be happy that you're bringing in a few bucks).

12. **Plan to finish on time.** The average student at a so-called four-year college now takes five or six years to finish. And many community college students take more than two years to complete their degrees. In most cases, it is financially advantageous to finish your degree in the allotted time. You'll surely save money if your school charges by the semester (rather than by the credit hour). And some four-year colleges even offer special discount rates, and promise never to raise the rates, if you sign onto a four-year-to-degree plan (sometimes called the eight-semester plan).

 BEST-KEPT SECRET. If you're short one or two courses, you can "buy" them at summer school, at a nearby community college, or, in some cases, at an online university. It'll be much cheaper and you won't have to sign up for a whole new semester.

The College Student's Bill of Rights

As a college student you don't just have responsibilities, you have rights. But figuring out what these rights are—and what they do and don't include—is often no simple matter. Here's our (semi-) humorous take on what you are—and aren't—entitled to at college:

Article 1. You have the right to annual tuition that is less than the price of a Lexus IS C convertible—at least the one that doesn't come with the HDD navigation system.

Article 2. You have the right to comprehensible, easy-to-fill-out FAFSA and Profile® forms—or at least ones that don't require a PhD from Wharton or Sloan School to get past page two.

Article 3. You have the right to affordable textbooks—that is, if you think $600 a semester is "affordable."

Article 4. You have the right to professors who are basically knowledgeable about the material—just not ones who can hold their own against Adderall in keeping you awake.

Article 5. You have the right to professors who sometimes offer up something funny—just not ones making regular appearances at WWW.COLLEGEHUMOR.COM.

Article 6. You have the right to a professor who dresses neatly and professionally—just not one who never wears "mom-jeans."

Article 7. You have the right to professors who don't hit on students— just not ones who rank a chili pepper at WWW.RATEMYPROFESSORS.COM.

Article 8. You have the right to adjunct instructors or TAs who are courteous, friendly, and nice—or at least would be if they were making enough to live indoors.

Article 9. You have the right to a "smart" classroom that is equipped with twenty-first-century technology—just not a prof who has any idea how to use the stuff.

Article 10. You have the right to nod off, zone out, or IM once in a while during lecture—but not the right to play Pocket Rockets on your iPhone right under your prof's nose.

Article 11. You have the right to express your views in discussion section—just not to hold court in your astronomy course on why the moon landing was a hoax.

Article 12. You have the right to an exam with questions reasonably related to what was talked about in class—just not one that covers only the classes you bothered to show up for.

Article 13. You have the right to dispute your paper grade and get a clear explanation of why you got the grade you did—just not to have your grade raised simply because "you paid good money for this stinkin' course." (We've heard this argument more times than we care to remember.)

Article 14. You have the right to get an extension on your paper if you have a serious medical emergency, a death in the family, or you wind up in jail (no kidding, it really happens)—but not if your Internet connection failed just as you were downloading page six from WWW.COLLEGEPAPERMILL.COM (not a real site, so don't bother).

Article 15. You have the right to talk to a professor about the term paper during his or her office hours—just not at 5:45 p.m. on the third Thursday of the month (the one time you can make given your jam-packed schedule of work, intramural sports, and hooking up).

Article 16. You have the right to a comfortable working environment in which to take your final exam—or at least enough space so that your classmate sitting next to you (who hasn't showered in three days) isn't pouring sweat onto your paper.

Article 17. You have the right to spaces in courses you need for your major—at least *some* time in the next seven years.

Article 18. You have the right to a seamless transfer of credits from a community college to a four-year college—in your dreams. (Get ready for hours of pitched battle when you try to transfer that graphic design 101 course you took back in 1994.)

Article 19. You have the right to professors who don't attempt to tell lame jokes—a right you can promptly exercise by turning the page.

2 IN THE BEGINNING...

There's always a huge amount to do when you're getting ready for the college year. Luckily, your to-do list needn't include recreating the heavens and the earth. Nevertheless, it can be quite long. Getting supplies for college, meeting your roommate, or planning your commute, picking your courses and getting used to them—all of these are part of the back-to-college grind. There's no need, however, to run around like a chicken without a head. Or to get so freaked out by what's to come that you end up paralyzed, unable to even start on what there is to do. Our tips will help you focus on what's most important at this time and guide you through the key decisions you'll need to make.

In this chapter you'll learn:

► 7 Things to Do the Summer Before College

► 15 Things to Do the Week Before College

► Do's and Don'ts for Picking Your Courses

► What to Do When You're Closed out of a Course

► 10 Questions to Ask Yourself the First Week of Classes

► The 13 Warning Signs of a Bad Professor

7 Things to Do the Summer Before College

Some students—and their parents—can't start on college soon enough. And it's a good thing. The more you do the summer before college, the less you have to do come crunch time, the week-before-college rush. To help all you early birds (and just about everyone else college-bound), here are our seven best things to do the summer before college:

1. **Get to orientation—early.** Almost all colleges offer summer orientation programs—typically day-long affairs, some as early as June, in which students and their parents can tour the campus, visit with a few faculty members and academic advisers, and, most important, pick their courses (hopefully it's the students doing the picking, not the parents). Many colleges follow the airline model: only a limited number of spaces, especially in large, required first-year courses that, when filled, are gone. Tip: go to the very first orientation session you can make, for your best shot at the courses you want.

 BEST-KEPT SECRET. If you get into an honors program, or declare your major, or (at some colleges) sign up for a four-year time-to-degree, you might qualify for special places reserved for these "privileged" classes of students. Find out if you're eligible.

2. **Get some hardware.** If you don't already have a computer, preferably a notebook, netbook, or tablet, now's the time to get one. Whether you choose a PC or Mac, we think your computer should weigh no more than three or four pounds, have at least a six-hour battery life (a must for taking notes in lectures throughout the day), have wireless capability, and have a full-size (or at least 92 percent of full-size) keyboard. (For our most current recommendations, including prices and where to buy, check out WWW.PROFESSORSGUIDE.COM/ TECHRECS.)

IOHO. If you're thinking of buying an e-reader, make sure it has highlighting, note-taking, and Internet capabilities. Those are features you're sure to want at college. (A color screen would be a nicety.)

3. **Get some software.** You'll also want to get some good word processing software. Microsoft Word 2007 is the college standard, though many students like the free OpenOffice alternative. (We won't be buying Word 2010 'til it has been around a while; new releases frequently have bugs.) If you're buying more task-specific software— say, for your business, graphic design, or urban planning course—we strongly recommend that you hold off until your course has started and your instructor tells you what to buy. It'd be a shame to spend $329 on the wrong program, only to find that it's nonreturnable.

4. **Surf the college Web site.** Sure, you've had a peek and watched the glossy propaganda videos when you were choosing a college. But now have a look at the academic side of things. Go to the college portal of the university you'll be attending; look for the *academics* or *for current students* tabs; then search for the *college requirements*, the list of *majors and minors*, the individual *departmental home pages* (where you might even find syllabuses for the courses offered), and the *course schedule* (the actual list of courses to be offered in the fall—not to be confused with the course *catalogue*, which is the list of every course ever offered). The more you know about the structure of the school, the easier it'll be to navigate once you get there.

5-STAR TIP. Master the academic calendar. It's worth checking out when classes start and end, when finals are held, the dates of those all-important fall and spring breaks, and whether your school celebrates Martin Luther King Day, Robert E. Lee Day, or Tu B'Shevat. Now's the time to make sure your parents don't schedule their twenty-fifth wedding anniversary, the family ski trip to Steamboat Springs, or the adoption of your new baby brother smack in the middle of final exam week.

5. **Dust off your language skills.** Most every college has a foreign language requirement, usually a four-semester sequence in a language of your choice. Now would be a good time to brush up on a language you learned in high school or speak around the house. If your summer plans include travel abroad, resolve to speak only the language of the country from touchdown to return home. Better language proficiency will not only save you some of the distribution requirements, it'll actually be a boon if you major in one of those fields that use foreign-language resources—European or Asian history, international marketing, Slavic literature, or premed or other health care professions.

 EXTRA POINTER. If your school assigns summer reading for the first-year experience course or the freshman seminar, plan to get it done. You don't want to be behind before the race has even started.

6. **Reach out to your roommate.** It's always a good idea to find out whom you're going to be sharing your digs with for the next nine months. If you're planning to live on campus, your college might be sending you all sorts of information about your assigned roommate; but even if they don't, you can check him or her out on your own. You don't have to scour WWW.BACKGROUNDCHECKS.COM or WWW.BEENVERIFIED.COM, since a simple Google search or glance at his or her Facebook page should give you more dirt—er, information—than you need. Once you get to know your new roommate a little—or if you're rooming with a good friend from high school or from previous years at college—it wouldn't be a half-bad time to make some "room rules": When do lights go on and off? What will the "do not enter (you wouldn't want to see what's going on in here)" signal be? And how much noise and partying is too much (or not enough)?

7. **Pursue your passion.** The summer before college is one of the last times you'll be able to do what you most enjoy doing, for 100 percent of the time. For Lynn, age seventeen, it was reading Russian novels. For Jeremy, age eighteen, it was working in a camera store.

And for our son Jonah, age twelve, it's designing bridges and reen-gineering the New York City subway system for greater efficiency. Getting in touch with your true passion—and cultivating it without the demands of school—will put you in a really good, and motivated, mood for college in the fall. And, with any luck, it'll net an elective course in Tolstoy, marketing, or civil engineering that you'll actually look forward to going to.

5-STAR TIP. The secret of college success is integration—lining up what you want to do with what you have to do. If you succeed at this, you will succeed at college.

15 Things to Do the Week Before College

The semester's just about to start. And you're all geared up for fifteen weeks of great courses. Or maybe you're still in vacation mode and haven't even had a thought about the semester that, now that you think of it, begins next week. Either way, you're guaranteed the best semester ever if you follow our fifteen must-do's for the week before college:

1. **Figure out where you're going and how you're going to get there.** Nothing at college is worse than discovering on the first day that there are no spaces left in Lot 32 or that the bus doesn't stop at Lincoln and Nebraska. Always have a Plan B. And while you're at it, figure out where your classes are going to meet. You wouldn't want to show up at 411 Old Main, only to find the class is at 411 New Main.

2. **Figure out where you're going to eat.** Are you going to be taking lunch to classes or going back to your dorm or apartment to eat? And what about Sunday nights, when (for who knows what reason) the food service in the dorms is closed? Hey, you can't do this college thing without proper nourishment.

3. **Plan an exercise routine.** Colleges invest gazillions of dollars in world-class exercise facilities. Go over to one of them, pick up a barbell, and imagine yourself doing this three times a week. (At least you'll have a sound body in which to put your, hopefully, sound mind.)

4. **Get some proper beverage equipment.** Every lecture or discussion section will go better with a piping hot caffeinated drink. So hoof on over to the local superstore or coffee bistro and buy the biggest spill proof stainless steel thermos you can find. Even if the lectures are not so hot, at least you'll be awake and not spilling coffee on the legs of your pants (or worse). (Non-coffee-drinkers should consider vitamin water and five-hour energy drinks).

5. **Buy the tomes.** Check out the textbooks and other required books at your campus bookstore (as well as other bookstores near

the campus). Also consider online sites (AMAZON.COM, BN.COM, EFOLLETT.COM, HALF.COM); book rental sites—by the month or semester (CHEGG.COM, CAMPUSBOOKRENTALS.COM, BOOKRENTER.COM); and even general merchandise sites (CRAIGSLIST.COM, EBAY.COM, and your college online newspaper).

EXTRA POINTER. If you're thinking of buying online, you might want to use metasites—Web sites that compare prices at many online booksellers. Some of the best are BIGWORDS.COM, BESTBOOKBUYS.COM, and CHEAPESTTEXTBOOKS.COM (some of these you can even get on your mobile phone). If you own a Kindle, Sony Reader, iPad, Entourage Edge, or other e-reader, be sure to consider e-textbooks. They can be cheaper and, no matter what, will be easier on your back. (For our latest e-book site and e-reader recommendations, including prices and where to buy, check out WWW.PROFESSORSGUIDE.COM/BOOKRECS.)

6. **Start calendaring.** Get a good electronic or print calendar and start entering your time commitments right away: when your classes meet, when you plan to study, what the assignments are, and when they're due (often these can be found in advance on the course Web page). Some of the e-calendars we like include Google Calendar, iStudiez, AirSet, 30 Boxes, and iCal (for Mac). Of course, if you have an iPad or iPhone, do your calendaring there.

7. **Learn to Skype.** If you've never tried real-time video conferencing, try out the free program at WWW.SKYPE.COM. You'll be able to talk to—and see—high school friends at other campuses, professors holding virtual office hours and individual conferences, and even your parents and siblings back home, if you're so inclined. (If your computer doesn't have a built-in Web cam and mic, you'll need to buy one for about $30 at your campus computer store.)

8. **Get the word.** You'll need a password to access the university portal (which is where you'll find course Web pages, library e-resources, your enrollment status and grades, and online registration in

semesters to come). Get it now. Also take advantage of your free university e-mail account: professors will be happier getting papers from jeremy.hyman@ucla.edu than from jeremythestud@ mondohotbodies.com.

9. **Visit the books—including the electronic ones.** Make your way over to the library and see where the books and journals are shelved. And while you're at it, look at the electronic resources at your library's home page: see how the databases and e-resources are organized and imagine yourself actually using them. With any luck, you will. (You'll find more details about this in "16 Techniques for Doing Research Like a Professor" on pp. 118–122.)

10. **Scout out the services.** When you have some extra time, make a campus tour and check out the various "offices": advising center; writing center; math and computer labs; tutoring center; and centers for nontraditional students, first-generation students, international students, single parents, and veterans. Hey, you've prepaid for all these offices; who knows, you might actually want to use one someday.

11. **Find yourself a cave.** You won't want to spend much time during the semester trying, then retrying, all kinds of study places. Figure out where you think you'll study best, then christen this place as your study spot.

12. **Rein in the folks.** Set some limits on your parents, especially if your dad—or mom—is the type who'll be texting you the two hours a day that he or she isn't calling you. And protect your Facebook page if your parents are the intrusive type—or if you think you'll have stuff going on that you don't want to become a family affair. You might prohibit them from posting messages on your wall or tagging you in family photos—or refuse to "friend" them altogether. (Of course, if they're paying for your college and they know the ins and outs about Facebook, your folks might not be all that happy about your banning them from your page.)

13. **Meet the prof.** For the really bold—especially at smaller, friendlier colleges—there's the visit to the professor's office to find out a little more about the course and distinguish yourself from the nameless

masses. Don't be put off, though, if the professor is too busy to visit with you (he or she might be rushing to polish off the syllabus or fig-ure out what to say in the first week of lectures).

14. **Go clubbing.** While you still have some free time, it's nice to see what kinds of student clubs and teams your college has to offer. You might just be dying to join the Jews for Jesus or the Wiccans, the Young Green Republicans or the Democrats for Sarah Palin, the Rock-Paper-Scissors Club or the Death Cab for Cutie fan club. And even if you don't want to join in on the fun, the look-over will give you a better feel for what's going on at the school and what the students are like.

15. **Take a breath.** Fifteen weeks is a long haul. Don't get wound up too quickly. There'll be plenty of time for panic once the semester sets in.

Do's and Don'ts for Picking Your Courses

One of the first orders of business in any new semester is picking—and getting settled into—your courses. The job can be both incredibly exciting and, especially if it's your first time (or even if it isn't), incredibly intimidating. It can seem like there are more choices than stars in the universe. And who really knows what they do in anthropology, linguistics, or communication studies—not to mention applied developmental psychology, geospatial information systems, and ichthyology (the study of fish, for the curious)? But have no fear. Follow our do's and don'ts, and you're sure to land the very best courses your college has to offer:

Do scour the college online catalogue—and the course page (when available)—for as much information as possible about what the course involves. In the best case, you'll find not only a detailed course description, but a list of the books to read, the assignments required, and even a course syllabus.

Don't just limit yourself to courses you know, like American history, English literature, or Spanish—or those courses recommended by an adviser as the "standard first-year program." One of the main points of going to college is to find out about things—even whole fields of knowledge—that you've never even heard about or that aren't required. Besides, you're probably tired of those old subjects, anyway, and you'll quickly get tired of all those requirements, too.

Do haul on over to registration (or, if you're just starting college, orientation) at the very first available time. Though we know you'd rather do just about anything else but face up to new classes, you'll guarantee yourself the best choice of classes and times if you're at the head of the line. Many popular, and some required, courses don't have enough places at some colleges, and, hey, it's a first-come, first-served world, especially in a time of overcrowding and cutbacks.

Do take the normal course load, perhaps even one that's a bit lighter than normal, if you can.

Don't load up with a basket of courses that would overwhelm even Hermione and her Time-Turner. There are no prizes for taking overloads, and while you might impress your dorm mates with the biggest course load ever, their admiration might fade as *you* start to fade by midterms.

Do carefully consider which foreign language to take—and at what level. Some languages are much harder than others—among the hardest are Arabic, Chinese, Japanese, and Russian (though these do offer better job potential). Once you've picked, in many schools you're stuck with four semesters of the stuff (more than virtually any other college sequence). *Quelle horreur*!

Don't overestimate—or underestimate—your level of knowledge in the language you took back in high school. If you have a good mastery of a language, don't go back to baby talk—the very first courses will bore you to tears. But if the best you can do in the foreign language is count to five—and you're not all that sure about four, come to think of it—you probably do want to sign up for whatever-language-it-is 101.

Do make sure to select the correct level math course for your background and ability. In our experience, more mistakes are made in signing up for math classes than in picking any other courses.

Don't assume that just because you got a 4 or 5 on the AP test that you're ready to take Math for Brainiacs. College courses—especially calculus—can have theory, which is good deal harder than figuring out areas under curves.

Do be aware that some departments, especially science departments, offer introductory courses designed specifically for majors in the field, and others (so-called "service courses") for students who'd "just like to learn a little something" (translation: pass the requirement) in that science. If you have a serious interest in a field or are thinking you might major in it, by all means take the intro for majors, not the sublevel service course that not only will bore you to tears, but won't count for the major when you get into it. (You wouldn't want to take two intros, would you?)

Don't take physics for majors if you really need to be in physics for poets—or drawing for art majors if paint-by-numbers is all the art you've ever done. The "majors" courses are not only going to be too hard, they're going to focus on all the boring, technical stuff you'd need to major in that field.

Do balance your program, choosing some courses that are easier, some harder, some that interest you, and some that fulfill requirements.

Don't listen to your parents or others telling you to "get all the requirements out of the way first." You'll suck the joy out of college and miss out on chances to take courses you might actually enjoy.

Do check out the first-year experience (FYE) course or freshman seminars (FSs). They're a great place to find out more about your college, polish up your skills, or read a book about globalization and the decline of American culture. And in many cases you'll get a real, breathing faculty member, not some TA or adjunct faculty person your college hired yesterday. (See "10 Tips for the First-Year Experience Course" on pp. 92–94 for more on FYE and FS courses.)

Bonus Do. If you're an upper-class student (a junior, senior, or sixth-year senior), be sure to consult with the undergraduate adviser in your department (rather than a general college adviser). Not only will he or she help you pick courses that'll best suit your program or interests within the field, he or she might offer you dirt about which profs will bore you to tears, which profs barely know their stuff, and which profs are teaching some course only because the chair of the department dumped it on them at the last moment. Your departmental adviser can be your best ally in picking courses.

No Room at the Inn? What to Do When You're Closed out of a Course

The crisis is nationwide. Public universities in economically distressed states (such as California, Arizona, Florida, Michigan, and Ohio) simply don't have enough space to accommodate all their students in all the classes they want. And with record enrollments, even some private colleges are feeling the squeeze. What's a student to do? Here are some things you might try if you're having trouble getting into the class you really want:

✔ **Pick an off-peak time.** Consider taking the sections that meet at times students find most undesirable. Think 7 a.m., late afternoons and evenings, and Fridays.

✔ **Wait it out.** Virtually all schools have wait lists, and many courses experience surprising drop rates in the first week or two—especially if the professor is bad or announces that the course will be curved or graded really hard. Even if you're fiftieth on the list, you can sometimes get in.

✔ **Come up with a really good reason you need the course.** Go over to the professor's office—during posted office hours (you'll find these on the syllabus, the course Web page [if any], and the card in front of the prof's office)—and explain, simply and without apology, your reasons for needing this course. Focus on academic reasons: you're a graduating senior, the course is a prerequisite for something you want to take next semester, your transfer from community college to state university would be held up without this course, or your senior thesis would benefit immeasurably from this course.

✔ **Wait 'til summer.** Many of the very same courses, often taught in smaller sections, are offered during summer session(s). Check out the university Web site to see if the course you can't get into is one of them.

✔ **Try a nearby school.** If your course is full at that four-year state university or private college, consider taking an equivalent course at a nearby community or city college. Just be sure the course is substantially similar in content and, more important, that the credits will transfer to your home institution.

✔ **Look for an online substitution.** Some high-tech and other over-loaded schools offer online versions—with a potentially unlimited number of places—of popular courses (especially math courses). See if your college has any of these.

✔ **Find another course to satisfy the requirement.** At many schools, distribution requirements are disjunctive—they can be satisfied by any one of a number of courses. Look for something almost as good (or better, because it has open spaces).

✔ **Appeal with a higher level course.** Some schools allow you to substitute a higher level course for an introductory or general education requirement. Talk to a departmental adviser to see if you can replace the closed-out course with something more advanced—for instance, *America in the 1960s* for *American History 1877 Through the Present.* In times of stress advisers often have special permission to make substitutions.

✔ **Look in your vault.** Sometimes you've already taken a course somewhere that could satisfy a requirement. Maybe an AP course, a course at some other college you once attended, or some "life experience" that could translate into some credit. Hey, an ace in the hole is an ace in the hole.

✔ **Beg (or at least cajole).** College professors and departmen-tal advisers sometimes have considerable discretion in giving "overrides" to deserving—or sometimes just plain nice—students. Think about what you'd like to hear from a student wanting to get into your class. Then go lay those things on the prof—only about three times as thick.

10 Questions to Ask Yourself the First Week of Classes

You might have thought that once you've picked your classes, you're over and done with it. The die is cast, now just settle in and enjoy your semester. But a far better idea is to size up the professor yourself, by attending the first few lectures and making your own judgment. After the very first class (or first couple of classes, if the first class is just an intro), ask yourself these ten questions about what you've just witnessed:

1. **Is the teacher good?** Even after the first class or two, you should be able to tell if the prof knows his or her stuff and can present the material in a clear, organized, and coherent manner—and whether the lecture has a point. A good teacher will construct each class around one or two main issues and make logical and clear transitions from point to point.

2. **Is the teacher interesting?** Look, college isn't Second City, so don't expect your molecular biology professor to have you rolling in the aisles with laughter. Still, your teacher should run the class in a way that holds your attention (at least most of the time); that makes the material real (or at least sort of relevant); and that displays some enthusiasm (or at least a few signs of life). Bonuses here could be an interesting use of media in the class, stimulating readings and assignments, and provocative discussion sessions.

3. **Does the teacher care that the students learn?** Signs that the professor cares include: a willingness to take questions, an awareness of how the students are receiving the material, and professor's showing respect when addressing students.

4. **Is the course too hard (or too easy)?** Sure, most college courses, especially first-year courses, are designed to introduce students to new subjects and different ways of thinking. But if you can't understand anything that's going on in the first few classes, this is a sign

that you are in over your head—something that's only going to get worse as the class gets deeper into the material. (On the other hand, if you've already had the material in some other class—or if the course is such a joke that even Bozo would be at the head of the class—well, why waste your time?)

5. **Does the course presuppose stuff you don't know?** Pay close attention if the professor or the course syllabus announces that you must have a particular skill (such as knowing differential calculus or being able to use AutoCAD) or have taken some prerequisite (for example, two semesters of university chemistry) before taking this course. Students who lack the skills or haven't taken the prereqs are likely to find themselves playing catch-up from Day 1, without ever really succeeding.

6. **Does the course have too much work?** The course syllabus should give you a pretty clear sense of how much reading, writing, and testing the course requires. There's nothing wrong with courses that are challenging; and learning to write well is one of the most important things you can accomplish in college. But you need to balance the requirements of this course with all your other commitments. If one course is so excessive it eats up all your waking hours, then, unless that course is ultraimportant for your major or your lifelong dream, you should drop it and look elsewhere.

7. **Would another course be a better choice for this requirement— or this major?** Colleges often give a wide variety of choices for the gen ed requirement. Don't feel obligated to take the most popular choices or only the courses you've heard of. So too for the requirements for your major. Often there is a different—and better—professor teaching the same required course that same semester or at least in the next semester.

8. **Do you really want to be learning this stuff at all?** Sometimes after looking over the syllabus and hearing the professor describe what he or she plans to do in the course, it's pretty clear that this isn't what you bargained for when you signed up. Like the student who signed up for critical reasoning, thinking she'd finally stop falling for her

boyfriend's lines and found herself doing truth tables and working to master *modus tolendo ponens* all semester long.

9. **Do you feel you can learn from this professor?** Every professor has a different teaching style, and some approaches may suit you better than others. Even if the professor has a great reputation and all your friends loved the course, it can still be taught in a way that doesn't fit your learning style. Don't be a lemming.

10. **Do you like the class?** In a good class, you should have some feeling of intellectual excitement and, yes, some enjoyment from the very beginning. If this feeling is absent at the start, it'll only get worse by the thirtieth lecture. Don't disregard your initial impression. If you don't like what you're seeing, drop the class and add another.

Warning! Bad Professor Ahead

Here are thirteen surefire signs that your prof's a dud—and that you should get out while there's still time:

1. **The professor is deadly boring.** Even in the very first classes, you can tell when it's a struggle to stay minimally conscious for the whole lecture. If you're bored to tears and need to text message nonstop, down a six-pack of Red Bull, or pinch yourself—hard—just to stay awake, you know something's not right here. (Hint: it's the professor.)

2. **The professor is bummed out.** If a professor comes in on the first day of classes already grumbling about how much he or she hates teaching this course, how much he or she would like to be teaching at a better college, or how teaching is a waste of his or her time (because research is where it's at), don't expect things to get any better as the course progresses. Rule of thumb: bummed out to start gets more and more bummed out as the weeks drag on.

3. **The professor is condescending, combative, or full of him- or herself.** Do you really want a professor who treats you like a five-year-old? Or thinks that students are the enemy, to be defeated in the pitched battle that is the course? Or that he or she is God's gift to student kind? Probably not.

4. **The professor shows favoritism.** Maybe he or she doesn't like students who have experience in the field (since they've already been corrupted or learned bad habits) or prefers majors or upperclasspeople (even though the course has no prerequisites). Or perhaps the professor has a cadre of students who keep taking his or her courses, so there's an in-crowd and an out-crowd before the class even starts. Since college courses aren't rock concerts, groupies shouldn't be part of the scene.

5. **The professor doesn't give out a syllabus—or gives out a one-paragraph syllabus that is just the course description from the Web.** Some professors say they want to let the course evolve, making careful adjustments based on the pace of the lectures, the speed at which students are doing the work, or the general ebb and flow of the semester. Right. More likely is that the professor who doesn't distribute a detailed syllabus doesn't actually know what he or she is going to be doing in the class this semester. Students in this course could well be buying a pig in a poke, which, of course, is not recommended.

6. **The professor isn't clear about the requirements and how much they count.** Professors who don't have a clear and easily expressible idea about how the grading will be handled can wind up springing all sorts of wacky systems or inconsistent grading schemes on the students as the semester progresses. Often students in this sort of class never know how they're doing during the semester and experience unpleasant surprises at the end.

7. **The professor has incredibly petty rules.** Bail out if you encounter a syllabus with page upon page of rules dealing with everything from the use of cell phones to whether you can wear caps to an exam; how to address the professor and when to ask questions; when you can enter the room and when you can leave; policies about eating, drinking, and using the bathroom; twenty-five acceptable reasons for an extension and fifty-three unacceptable reasons; grade penalties for lateness timed to the half hour, and so on. Sure, some rules are required by the school (due dates, grading policy, and, in cold climes, even snow policy), but the prof's supposed to be teaching a course, not rewriting the health care system.

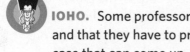 **IOHO.** Some professors will tell you the syllabus is a contract and that they have to protect themselves against every possible case that can come up. But the atmosphere they create by doing this is so combative that a shared learning experience is unlikely to emerge.

8. **The professor can't fill the whole class period.** Lots of professors hold a short class the first day of classes: they introduce themselves, go over the syllabus, and call it a day. But if class is let out early the whole first week, you can be pretty sure that the professor is either inexperienced, a bad planner, or, worst of all, doesn't really give a damn about the course. Sure, you'd like to blow it off early every day. But why cheat yourself out of the education you've paid for?

9. **The professor seems unsure about the material.** Professors who present their lectures in a halting or tentative way could well be professors who aren't on top of the course content. You might think that colleges would only hire people who really know the material backward and forward, but you'd be wrong. It's not at all uncommon for faculty to be saddled with a course in which they have no expertise. Why should you be saddled with it too, when you've got a choice?

 IOHO. If the professor says he or she is going to "learn the material with you," get out as fast as you can. That's professor-speak for "I don't know my a** from my elbow about this stuff."

10. **The professor presents the material in a confused or obscure way.** If your professor's lectures wander aimlessly through lots of unrelated details—or if the professor seems to be just dumping everything he or she knows about the topic without making any of it clear or understandable—something is definitely wrong. Like that the professor isn't able to explain the stuff in a way the students can understand—or, in street language, that he or she can't teach.

11. **The professor uses the class as a political platform.** Even if the class is a political science or government course, the professor should not be using the lecture to spout off on his or her own political views. If your prof wants to be a politico, let him or her go on O'Reilly or Olbermann.

12. **The professor never involves the students.** If a professor attends only to his or her notes and never even looks at the students—or never pauses to accept or invite questions—it's not a good thing. A

good class is a dynamical class, and a good professor engages with the students.

13. **The professor has no passion for the subject.** If the professor is just slogging through the material with no apparent enthusiasm for anything he or she has to say—well, how are you supposed to get excited (or even at all interested) in what's about to go on? Find a prof who's engaged with his or her material—and with teaching it to you.

3

SKILLS 3.0

Being successful at college requires a full array of skills. Some come into play at key moments in the semester, like when you're facing major tests and papers (more on these in Chapter Five). Others are needed throughout the term. Let's face it, on most days you have to go to class, do the assigned reading, and/or study for some weekly quiz. That's why it's important to have the skills of college down cold. Part of the day-to-day routine of your life.

For many college students, this is more of a dream than a reality. Sure, they've learned Skills 1.0, the first-generation level of studying, managing their time, and taking tests that everyone learns in high school. Some have even mastered Skills 2.0, the second-generation level of skills that, with any luck, you've perfected in your first year of college. But do you know what it'd be like to have third-generation skills—fully polished, professional abilities that'll drive you to the top of your college class and lead to a great career?

In this chapter you'll learn:

- ▶ Top 10 Time-Management Tips
- ▶ Why It's Never Good to Procrastinate
- ▶ How *Not* to Study
- ▶ 10 Secrets of Taking Excellent Lecture Notes
- ▶ 15 Ways to Read Like a Pro
- ▶ 15 Strategies for Painless Presentations
- ▶ How to Build Your Confidence at College

Top 10 Time-Management Tips

College is like juggling: five balls in the air, trying not to let any of them drop. Between going to class, doing the homework, taking the tests, perhaps holding down a job or raising a family—well, how's a mere mortal supposed to do all this stuff? It boils down to managing your time: figuring out where each commitment is supposed to go, deciding how much time to apportion to each, and, most of all, staying on track for the whole fifteen-week semester. But how are you supposed to do all that? Here are our top ten tips for managing your jam-packed schedule:

1. **Block your courses.** Many students think they'll learn better if they scatter their courses throughout the day with frequent downtime. Wrong. Usually, if you have a gap of fifty minutes between classes, it's much more likely to end up as Twitter or Facebook time than as study time. If you take your courses back to back as much as possible, you'll have larger blocks of time to devote to concerted bouts of studying. And if you can group your classes on only two or three days, it will free whole days for studying.

2. **Make a plan.** It's never too early to start figuring out how you'll do all the work in each of your four or five classes. In fact, the very first day of classes is the right time. Enter all the assignments—including weekly assignments, quizzes, and exercises or short papers—into your electronic or print calendar. Then develop an overall plan for both your run-of-the-mill weekly studying and the mondo research paper or killer final. Enter it all in or write it all out: no one can juggle in their head.

3. **Aim to make all the classes.** Going to classes is one of the most time-efficient things you can do. When you miss class, it takes three times as long to learn the material on your own as it would have taken to go to the lecture. And you never really learn it as well. Who could, getting notes from that classmate who writes illegibly and didn't really understand the lecture him- or herself?

4. **Determine whether you're an owl or a rooster.** Schedule your study-ing for times when you can seriously engage with the work. Depend-ing on their biochronology, some students find 11 p.m. the perfect time to focus, while others like 6 a.m. Just because your classmate studies at a particular time doesn't mean it will work for you.

EXTRA POINTER. Be sure to schedule time for sleep. Whether you study in the depths of night or at the crack of dawn, you'll need seven or eight hours of sleep. What good is it managing your waking time if you're so wasted that you can't concentrate on what you're doing?

5. **Set up "zones."** Many students have a lot things on their plate other than college—a part- (or full-) time job, a few kids to take care of, responsibilities at the church. It's a good idea to divide up your week, and your day, into different, and nonoverlapping time blocks. If you work at your job in the morning, then be sure to schedule all your courses and study time in the afternoons and evening. Tuesday and Thursday are your child care days? Don't try to prepare for your Friday test in those time blocks. The key to success when you have multiple commitments is compartmentalization: keep each activity separate, and don't let one zone bleed into another.

5-STAR TIP. Learn to say no. If you're in your study zone and your boss calls, or your kid needs help with his or her homework, or your pastor asks you for help with the pancake breakfast, tell them you'll get back to them later. Hey, your work should be at least as important as filling in for the sick worker, fifth-grade social studies, or the toppings for the pancakes.

6. **Keep a daily log.** Especially at the beginning of the semester, you should track how long it takes you to do the homework in each of your classes, to prepare for quizzes and tests, and to write short papers. Knowing this can help you estimate the time frame for future course assignments. Also, writing it down will prevent you from overestimating how long you're really studying (at least if you're recording honestly).

5-STAR TIP. Adjust your study plan dynamically as the semester progresses. Typically, you'll find that some courses get harder as they go, that some projects take longer than you planned, and that the workload is divided unevenly over the semester in some courses. The more flexible—and the more open-minded—you are about time management, the more successful you will be.

7. **Do your homework on time.** Even though there's no parent or teacher to stand over you, be sure you're doing the outside-of-class work when it's assigned. Doing the reading in advance of the lecture, studying for each quiz as it comes along, and memorizing what needs to be memorized on a week-by-week basis are all strategies that will increase your efficiency and cut down on overall study time. Sure, it's tempting to blow off the homework when there's no test looming or when the prof doesn't bother to call on anyone in class. But the fun will quickly diminish when you have five hundred pages of reading to catch up on two days before the test.

8. **Prioritize your study time.** Every professor thinks that his or her course is the most important thing in the universe. Learn to *triage* your courses—that is, to spend different amounts of time on each course depending on how important or difficult that course is. Do not spend all your time on the course you find most enjoyable or easiest to do. And if you find you're spending every waking hour on one of your courses, cut back. Keep in mind that you've signed up for four or five courses, each of which will count toward only 20 to 25 percent of your overall GPA.

9. **Plan to do each task once.** It's very time-inefficient to do things twice. Some students think they'll learn better by copying their notes over (more neatly this time), listening to the same lecture twice (once

in person, once on their iPod), or doing the reading three times (once to get the general idea, once to focus in on the plot and characters, and once to take notes). Fuggetaboutit. All these are incredible time wasters. And it's not likely that you'll be able to focus or understand better the second time around.

REALITY CHECK. At the end of the second week, assess whether you've had any do-overs—that is, done any task twice. If you find that you have, diagnose your problem and devise a strategy for doing each task once for the balance of the semester.

10. **Divide and conquer.** Break up larger projects such as research papers, field studies, and studying for cumulative exams into manageable chunks. And spread the stages over a reasonable number of days. Always add some extra time to what you think you need, because usually there's a major crunch or crisis toward the end. It's better to finish a little early than to find yourself running around like a madman when your computer crashes at 4 a.m. the morning before a paper is due.

Why It's Never Good to Procrastinate

Procrastinate *v.* To put off doing something until a future time [Latin *prōcrāstināre*, "to put forward until tomorrow"]

Tempted to put off studying for the particle physics test? Or writing that thirty-five-page research paper on future uses of nanotechnology? Sure you are? And who wouldn't be? But it's still a dumb idea. Here's why...

▶ **Tomorrow won't be better.** It'll still be the same task. It won't be any more fun and you still won't want to do it.

▶ **It only gets worse.** As the deadline gets closer and closer, the task starts to loom larger and larger if you haven't started the work. And the stress mounts. Now not only do you have to write that dreaded paper, you have to do it under the influence of your fight-or-flight hormones (which are designed to help you escape from a saber-toothed tiger and aren't of as much use when you're attempting to write coherent prose).

▶ **You're probably overestimating the pain.** Before you start, the task seems insurmountable, the pain immense. But you know what? You're probably miscalculating. Get started—maybe on a small piece—and you'll discover that you have more resources and know more about the subject than you thought. Result? You won't experience nearly as much suffering as you expected to.

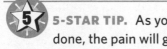 **5-STAR TIP.** As you whittle down the amount of stuff to be done, the pain will go down. So the amount of pain and resistance that you're feeling before you start is the maximum. Things are guaranteed—100 percent—to get better.

▶ **Ideas need time to jell.** Most college essays require you to have some kind of idea, then to spend some time thinking about it, revising it, and refining it. When you throw together a paper or a report at the last minute, your ideas are half-baked. And your professor will know it.

BEST-KEPT SECRET. Ever wonder why the professor assigns the paper two weeks before it's due? It's because he or she expects you to be thinking about the issue, or doing the research, for two weeks. No, not every waking moment, but at least some of the time. After all, the prof could just as easily have given the assignment one week before it was due if he or she expected less thinking.

▶ **You might be playing with less than a full deck.** After a professor assigns a paper topic, he or she often brings up material in class designed to help you with the assignment. But if you haven't even begun to think about the assignment, you might not even notice. Wonder how this might go? Let's say you haven't started on your paper and don't even realize that all the choices are about the Civil War. The prof gives the next two lectures on the causes of and battles in the Civil War, and, since the paper isn't even on your radar screen, you zone out during the class or blow it off altogether. Net result? Your procrastination has caused you to miss important clues about what could go into your paper. Shoulda started earlier.

▶ **You blow off your chances for help.** If you leave your work until the night before it's due, you give up the possibility of getting input from your prof or TA. Professors regularly dispense sage advice—or at least a few useful tips—during office hours. Unfortunately, though, they don't usually hold office hours at midnight, so you'll be out of luck when you discover the night before the midterm that you have no idea how to do the questions that will count for two-thirds of your grade.

▶ **You put yourself at a strategic disadvantage.** While you're find-ing reasons to put things off for another day, some of your cohorts have already burst out of the starting gate—even those duplici-tous traitors who assure you that they haven't cracked a book. These classmates will end up making you look bad, especially if the professor curves the grades.

▶ **Time can run out.** If you put things off 'til the last minute, you might find that you haven't budgeted enough minutes to finish the necessary tasks. It's the easiest thing in the world to misestimate how long it'll take to do all the stuff—especially when new issues arise as you're thinking through your paper argument or sketching out answers to possible test questions.

BONUS TIP. S*** happens. When you procrastinate, you don't allow yourself time for those various life events that adversely affect your ability to complete your assignment—like illness, family problems, computer breakdowns, trouble at work, and all the other things that seem to happen just as the deadline looms large.

The How *Not* to Study Guide

For many students, the biggest difference between college and high school is studying. In college you're supposed to do it, whereas in high school— well, you know, not really. But by the time they've gotten to college, many students have developed study habits and strategies that not only don't help them get ahead at college, they actually thwart their progress. For them—and perhaps even for you—we offer our fifteen best ideas for how *not* to study:

1. **Don't spend too much time looking for the perfect environment.** Many students think that if only they found the perfect place to study, it would all be a cakewalk. So they spend inordinate amounts of time scouting and trying out various locales—first their dorm room, then the coffee shop, then the library, then the grass, and so on. Such elaborate setup time can be a major time-waster, and, even worse, can make you feel that you can't study unless you are in your ideal study spot. Better idea? Find a reasonably quiet place and just get started. You'll get more comfortable with your surroundings as you get going.

2. **Don't multitask.** Believe it or not, some students study for *all* their courses at one session: fifteen minutes on this subject, fifteen minutes on another, fifteen minutes on a third—you get the picture. It's a far better idea to devote your entire study session to a single subject. That way, you'll build up speed, and, the more engaged you get, the easier the studying will become. Worst of all is to intersperse one subject with another—do ten minutes of math, then give up and do ten minutes of freshman comp, then back to the math. That's a recipe for guaranteed confusion.

3. **Don't count busywork as studying.** Some students do a lot of preparing or getting organized for studying, but they never get down to doing the actual studying. Don't give yourself credit for studying when you're actually just cleaning your desk, getting together the readings, or reorganizing the files on your laptop.

4. **Don't start with the no-brainers.** Some students think that starting with the easiest tasks—or the ones they're best at—will "ease them into" the material. Trouble is, when you get to the harder tasks, you still have the leap to make—and you're more tired, too. Suggestion: start with the hardest or most challenging task, then ease into the easier ones.

5. **Don't discard the clues.** Many professors give study questions, or at least say in class or on the syllabus what will be most important in the reading. Be sure to consider these all-important (and time-saving) suggestions before you start studying. If yours is a class with math problems or proofs, be sure to consult the problems done in lecture or section before taking off on the new ones. Often the homework problems are variants or extensions of the work already done.

6. **Don't just memorize.** It's useless to just shovel stuff into your mind that you don't understand. If you really are understanding what you're studying, you ought to able to explain the main ideas, in your own words, to someone who hasn't done the studying. Take the time to think about and digest what you're studying, instead of just preparing to parrot it back on some upcoming exam.

7. **Don't microfocus.** Some students think the best studying is slow studying: reading every word, one by one; writing every word of the paper, one by one; preparing a presentation, one word at a time. But like any cognitive activity, studying is a process that takes place over time and gains strength by building up speed. If you focus too narrowly on the individual elements of what you're doing, you suck the life out of the learning and disrupt the intellectual growth that's possible, even in studying.

EXTRA POINTER. Many students don't bother taking reading notes—or indeed any notes—thinking they'll remember what they studied come test time. No one can. Especially when you're taking four or five other courses. Tip: write down notes—on a clean sheet of paper, not in the margins of the book where you'll never be able to read them—as you read. Be sure to leave space for additional comments that you'll add when you go over your notes later in the semester.

5-STAR TIP. If you've invested in e-books and an e-reader that has note-taking and highlighting capabilities, it might be a good idea to take notes in the (electronic) margins. Those will be neat, and changeable, too, should you want to alter what you've written come study time.

8. **Adjust your attention span.** You're used to getting your content in 140-character units, in twenty-second bursts, or with lots of video to go with it. But college is not Twitter, YouTube, or Hulu. When studying in college, sustained attention is needed. Learn to focus—without breaks and without additional stimulation—for fifteen- to twenty-minute units. Look, we know it's hard to reprogram your brain. But doing so will prevent your having to start focusing again—and overcoming your resistance—fifty times an hour.

 EXTRA POINTER. Be sure you do take breaks from time to time. Giving your mind time to rest will keep up your stamina and, in addition, give ideas time to sink in. Rule of thumb: for every forty-five to fifty minutes of studying, allow a ten- to fifteen-minute break.

9. **Don't count "study" time as study time.** Some students keep three windows open while they read their e-textbook: one for the book, another for Facebook, and the third for Twitter (Windows 7 makes this easy). And then they flit back and forth from screen to screen, counting all the time as study time. When you're counting up your study time, count only the time you actually engaged with the material (not just the time you sat at your study place). If you can't do this honestly in your head, write it down. The pencil never lies.

10. **Don't count a "study" group as a study group.** Many classes have required or optional study groups in which you get together with other students from the same course to go over the material. If you're participating in one of these, make sure you and your friends

are actually studying the material, not just each other. If for whatever reason you're not studying the material, have a nice time—just don't count the time as study time.

11. **Don't be too hard on yourself.** Many students set elaborate study schedules—nothing wrong with that—and then beat themselves up when things don't go according to plan—not such a hot idea. Maybe some task took longer than anticipated, maybe some additional materials were needed to complete the task, or maybe you were just tired or distracted that day. Don't be too hard on yourself when you haven't stuck 100 percent to your plan. Keep in mind that you'll have many study sessions and that remaining in a positive mood about your schoolwork is much more important than how any one study session—or indeed series of sessions—goes.

12. **Don't go it alone.** If in spite of your very best efforts you find your-self spending enormous amounts of time preparing for one class or are always hopelessly behind in your studying for that class, go see the prof or TA. They've had loads of experience with students just like you, and they can make practical suggestions about how you can get on the right track. (For some tips on how to approach the professor, see "The 15 Secrets of Going to See the Professor" on pp. 129–133.)

13. **Never blow off two days in a row.** Though nobody quite tells you this, you're supposed to be studying every day of the week at col-lege. If each professor expects you to be preparing a couple of hours for each lecture hour, and if you're taking fifteen hours of lecture a week, you're supposed to be preparing thirty hours a week. Hard to fit thirty hours of studying in only three days a week, especially if you have lectures on those days.

14. **Don't cheat yourself.** To get the true value out of college, you'll have to be doing a lot of work on your own. If you don't study—or if you don't study well—you're only cheating yourself. Why do that?

10 Secrets of Taking Excellent Lecture Notes

Taking really good lecture notes is one of the most important skills for college success. Not only will constant writing help you stay awake and focused on the main points of the lecture, your lecture notes can become quite important come midterm or final time. Most college students think they're pretty good at note taking. Only one in ten is. Wonder how you can become that one? Have a look at the ten secrets of excellent note taking, all from the professors' perspective:

1. **Write more, not less.** You should be writing for most of the lecture. Sure, it's a question of balance and emphasis—getting enough down so that you've captured most of the detail, while highlighting the main points so you can see how the lecture is structured. But in our experience, it's far more common for students to have written down not nearly enough than to have written down far too much. Rule of thumb: fifteen minutes of lecture should produce one page of notes (or, in other words, three to four pages of notes for a typical hour of lecture).

2. **Use any advance information.** If the professor has given a title to each lecture on the syllabus or has given out study questions in advance of each lecture, make sure you familiarize yourself with these before coming to class. The more you know about what the main points of the lecture are going to be, the easier it will be to take notes. You'll know what you're looking for.

 5-STAR TIP. If the professor hasn't bothered to give each lecture a title, you should. That'll force you to locate the single most important point of that class.

3. **Write down the professor's ideas, not yours.** Some students lard their notes with their own questions, reflections, opinions, and free associations. But the point of taking notes is to get a good rendition of what the professor is saying. That's what'll be on the test. Leave your own thoughts for afterward or for your personal journal.

4. **Forget about complicated note-taking "systems."** Contrary to what they tell you, there's no need to use the Cornell Note-Taking System, Mind Mapping, or the "Five R's of Good Note Taking" (whatever they may be). It's more than enough to simply number the professor's points (and perhaps have a sub number or two). Worrying about systems will only slow you down and can distort the actual shape of the lecture. There's always time to go back later and structure your notes.

EXTRA POINTER. When taking notes, be sure to set off subordinate points (that is, points that contribute to the lecture in some way, but are not on the main path). Also, indent and clearly identify any illustrations, examples, comparisons, and interesting (though not central) asides. Be sure to note their relation to the main points.

5-STAR TIP. Whenever a professor uses a technical or unfamiliar term, be sure to write down—in the best case, word for word—the prof's definition of that term. These terms can play a critical role in later lectures and on the tests and papers.

5. **Don't zone in and out.** You're used to rapid-fire content delivered in twenty-second bursts. But the professor is used to dishing up his or her ideas in fifteen- to twenty-minute segments. Train yourself to focus—and to write—for longer intervals. Above all, don't be distracted by other activities that may be going on around you in the lecture hall—or on your iPhone, iPad, or Game Boy.

6. **Pay special attention to the beginning and the end.** Often the most important parts of the lecture are the first two minutes and the last two minutes, right when many students are shuffling in their seats or packing their bags. Many professors start their lectures by reviewing the key points of the last lecture and listing the main points they're going to cover in this lecture. And they conclude the class with a summary of the main points they have covered and sometimes an indication of what they'll do next time. Be sure to take careful notes during these high-value moments.

7. **Look for verbal clues.** Professors often try to flag the most important points in the lecture with phrases like "the key point is...," "it's especially important to note that...," and "one should keep in mind that..." Look for these indicators of the cornerstones of the lecture. And try to write down—word for word, if you can—the material that follows them.

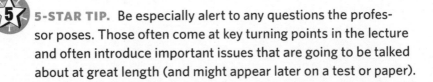

5-STAR TIP. Be especially alert to any questions the professor poses. Those often come at key turning points in the lecture and often introduce important issues that are going to be talked about at great length (and might appear later on a test or paper).

8. **Focus on the structure.** Every lecture has a plot: a central point with a series of steps that build up this point. Keep focused on the plot— and its subplots—and try to capture them in your notes. Continually ask yourself: *What is the overall point of the lecture? How does each individual point contribute to the overall plot? Why did the professor choose to make these points rather than others?*

9. **Beware of PowerPoints.** PowerPoints (and things written on the board) are usually quite sketchy outlines—reminders to the professors of what to say. Make sure you write down the explanations of these outlines in your notes, not just the outlines themselves. Come test time, you'll be behind the eight ball if all you have in your notes are these prompts the professor uses.

EXTRA POINTER. Take notes at all class activities—discussion sections, field trips, visits to the museum, review sessions, individual meetings in office hours—not just lectures. You never know what might come in handy when the test or paper comes around.

10. **Always do it yourself.** Don't outsource your note taking to your friend, to the professional "lecture notes" (sold at the campus store), or to your note-taking group. Taking notes for yourself is the single best way to engage in—and remember—the lecture. Not to mention it'll actually get you to go the lecture, which is an achievement in itself.

15 Ways to Read Like a Pro

One of the main skills to be mastered at college is college-level reading. Sure, you've been reading since you were five years old, but do you read fast enough for college? Do you not only get the plot, but analyze the characters and themes as you read? And for scientific and technical reading, are you really following—and evaluating—the theories, methods, and techniques the author is using, as well as the conclusions he or she is reaching? Maybe not? Here are our fifteen best tips to get you reading like an A+ student:

1. **Don't think you're the only one.** Don't blow off the reading on the theory that no one else is doing it. Plenty are—and you don't want them carting off all the good grades, do you?

2. **Decide what's required.** Figure out how much the professor is expecting you'll read. Usually, when there are exact pages specified, he or she's thinking you'll read them all. But when dozens of books are listed for a single week, the professor might be thinking you'll read "in" those books or select from among them. Don't do more—or less—than you need to do.

 IOHO. Pay special attention to the distinction between *required* reading and *recommended* (or supplemental) reading—that is, between what you absolutely, positively, 100 percent have to read, and what would be nice to read if only you had the time. We suggest that you stick to the required reading unless there's some special reason for doing the recommended reading (for instance, when it's relevant to your paper topic or you just happen to be interested in that issue—hey, it could happen).

3. **Figure out the point of the reading.** You'll understand the reading a whole lot better and enjoy it more when you know its purpose. Is the reading just general background? Is it the object to be studied in the lecture? Or does it go beyond what the professor is talking about, filling in gaps in the lecture? Figure out what the reading's supposed to be doing, and you'll know better how to do it.

4. **Always read *before* the class.** In most classes, it works best if you do the reading before you go to lecture. That's because most often the professor is expecting you to have done the legwork before he or she does the heavy lifting. And when the task of the lecture is to actually analyze the reading, it's particularly helpful to have read what's going to be analyzed. (Of course, if your professor tells you to read only *after* the lecture, follow his or her advice.)

5. **Let the professor be your guide.** Before starting the reading assignment, make sure you've checked out all the clues the professor has given about what you're supposed to be looking for in the reading. Study questions, comments in the previous lecture, handouts, things the TA says in section—all of these can contain hints that will make you a more probing reader. Also, be sure to pay special attention to any clues the author offers about what the key issues are. Titles, section headings, summaries, and any big proclamations ("In this section, I will show that...") can be enormously helpful in locating the points that the author thinks you should be focusing on.

6. **Think about it right.** Different kinds of reading materials require different kinds of reading. When you are reading a textbook, the main idea might be to get a general overview of the material and take in some basic facts. When you are reading an article, the point might be to study and evaluate the claims made by the author. When reading a novel or epic, you might be expected to analyze the character of the hero or assess the importance of various events. Look at how the professor is treating the reading in lecture, and try to mimic his or her methodology in your own reading.

7. **Track the developments.** In any reading—be it a textbook, scholarly article, novel, or a play—there's some building up of what the author has to say. As you read through the material, ask yourself: *How is the*

argument (or plot or story) developing? Why does this point follow the one that precedes? What work is it doing? The more you can see why the ideas are ordered in the way they are, the easier it'll be for you to understand the point of it all.

8. **Stop and think.** If you come to something you don't understand (especially if it seems important), don't just put your head down and charge forward. Stop and puzzle it out. In many college readings, what comes after depends on what comes before. If you don't understand what comes before, you won't understand what comes after.

9. **Use a dictionary.** Missing a key term—especially when it's a technical term or a strategically located word—can cause you to not understand what's said from that point on. Always have a dictionary of some sort (whether print, online, or even a cell phone app) when you sit down to read.

10. **Work the problems.** If yours is a math, science, or logic book, you should do the problems in your head as you're reading them. That way you won't just be passively absorbing what the author is saying, you'll be exercising your mind and applying the concepts to the material on your own. Just like you'll have to do on the test.

11. **Maintain the right pace.** While different kinds of reading go at different speeds, it's important never to adopt the pace of the snail or go at it like a bat out of hell. A good pace is one slow enough to really understand what's being said, but not so slow that you've squeezed any life out of what you're reading, or totally lost any overall sense of what's going on.

12. **Use a card.** The single best way to improve your reading speed is to physically move an index card the width of the page down the page as you read. This technique forces your eye to make fewer fixations on each single line, and propels your eye forward so you move through the page more quickly.

13. **Never sub-vocalize.** Contrary to what they might have taught you in first grade, reading out loud to yourself is a surefire way to slow yourself down. You're supposed to move directly from reading to

understanding, not through an intermediate stage of saying each word to yourself.

IOHO. Avoid methods like the SQ3R strategy that encourage you to do an activity out loud in your head. When you're reading fluidly, understanding should be automatic, not sub-vocalized.

14. **Read the extras.** Be sure to look at "gray boxes," illustrations, and problems solved in the reading. Even if they look pretty, they still count as content to master. And if the author has included "questions for thought" at the end of the chapter (especially in a textbook), you'd be a fool not to try to answer them, at least in your head.

15. **Keep a record.** Though we're not dead set against highlighting or writing code words in the margins, we think it's best to keep reading notes in a separate notebook or Word file (unless you're using an e-reader with good note-taking capacities). Come the test, it's three times as easy to study from a complete document as it is to scan a highlighted textbook that looks more like a Christmas tree than a summary of the reading.

BONUS TIP. Don't have a cow if the reading is not coming easily. Reading is a skill, and in many courses—especially ones in which you're new to the subject—you'll build up your comprehension and speed as the semester goes on. Keep at it, don't get depressed, and pretty soon you'll be reading as if you'd been doing it all your life. Which you have.

15 Strategies for Painless Presentations

Even more than death and taxes, the thing people fear most is speaking in public. Needless to say, college students are not immune from this terror—which, for you psychology hounds, even has a name: *glossophobia*. Unfortunately, at college it's not always so easy to avoid public speaking. Some schools have required courses in speech, while others incorporate reports, presentations, and seminars into a broad variety of courses. Still, there's no need to lose your breakfast (or lunch, dinner, or late-night snack) over your upcoming presentation. Our fifteen tips for improving your public speaking will make even a garden-variety speaker into a real Cicero:

1. **Do your homework.** Nobody can give a good presentation without putting in some serious time preparing his or her remarks. Many gifted speakers look like they're just talking off the cuff, saying whatever comes to mind. But in truth they've spent considerable time in advance figuring out what they're going to say. You should, too.

 5-STAR TIP. It's always a good idea to try out (at least part of) your presentation on your professor or TA before giving it in class. Office hours work well for this.

2. **Play the parts.** Good presentations are structured in sections. Organizing your points into two or three main parts—and telling your audience what these parts are (both at the beginning of the paper and at the start of each section)—can make the difference between a winning presentation and a loser.

3. **Do a dry run.** It's always good to do a run-through (or even a couple of run-throughs) the night before the presentation. This can help with both your timing and manner of presentation (be sure to make

mental notes if you went on too long or got nervous or stuck). Some people find it useful to have a friend pretend to be the audience. He or she can build up your confidence and maybe even ask a question or two (nothing wrong with trying your luck at interacting with a questioner).

4. **Look presentable.** No need to wear a suit, but it's hard for people to take a presentation seriously when you look like you've just rolled out of bed. Even if you have.

5. **Arrive early.** Even the most experienced speakers can come unglued if they have to rush through their setup—assembling their materials, preparing any handouts or displays, and simply getting in the proper frame of mind for a presentation. Give yourself a few extra minutes.

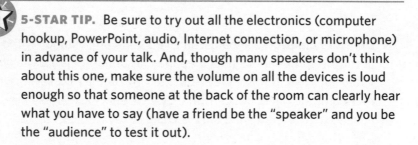

5-STAR TIP. Be sure to try out all the electronics (computer hookup, PowerPoint, audio, Internet connection, or microphone) in advance of your talk. And, though many speakers don't think about this one, make sure the volume on all the devices is loud enough so that someone at the back of the room can clearly hear what you have to say (have a friend be the "speaker" and you be the "audience" to test it out).

6. **Talk, don't read.** Nobody enjoys seeing a speaker burying his or her face in a script, reading stiffly. Try to talk from notes or, if you use a written-out text, try to look down at it only occasionally. Keep in mind that, in many cases, it's more important that you demonstrate an understanding of your topic than that you capture your prepared text word for word. (Your practice sessions should help you here, since they enable you to better remember what you want to say.)

7. **Take it slow.** The single biggest mistake inexperienced speakers make is going too fast. Remember that your audience is hearing the material for the first time and isn't nearly as familiar with it as you are.

EXTRA POINTER. If you find yourself running out of time, either drop, or briefly summarize, any left-over material. If your presentation includes a discussion period, gesture at the points you haven't fully covered and suggest them as things that could be discussed later.

8. **Use "aids."** For certain sorts of presentations, visual aids—such as PowerPoints, handouts, even things written on the board—can help your audience locate and grasp the main points and help *you* remember what they are. Just be sure you fully explain these materials in your presentation: no one is happy to see an outline that he or she can't make heads or tails of.

 EXTRA POINTER. Some presenters find the "speaker notes" feature in PowerPoint useful (you see a window with your notes that the audience doesn't see). Sure beats flash cards.

9. **Don't bury the crowd.** Including massive numbers of quotes or unfathomable amounts of data can overwhelm even the most attentive audience. Why would you want to do that?

10. **Be yourself.** As important as the content you present is your authenticity in presenting it. So don't try to be someone you're not. You'll never succeed.

11. **Play it straight.** There's no harm in including a little humor in your presentations, especially if you can carry it off well. But in most college presentations, clowns get C's.

12. **Circle the crowd.** A very important part of public speaking is to make eye contact with people seated in all parts of the room—even those nodding off in the back. This shows people that you're interested in communicating with them—not just getting through this hellish experience ASAP. And it wouldn't hurt to get out from behind the podium or desk, and walk around the room a little. Sharing space

with the audience can also communicate your interest in sharing your results with them—something you surely want to do.

13. **Appear relaxed.** You don't have to actually be relaxed—few speakers are—but at least try to appear as relaxed as possible. Bring along some water or a soft drink, take short breaks from time to time, and get absorbed in the moment. No one enjoys speakers who are trembling and sweating bullets.

14. **Finish strong.** Always be sure to have a satisfying conclusion to your presentation, in which you make clear to the listeners what they now know. This creates a warm feeling in the minds of your listeners and shows them that they've really learned something from your lovely talk.

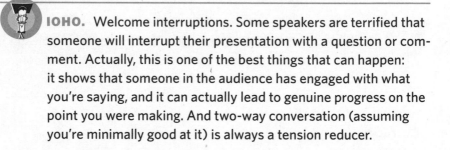

IOHO. Welcome interruptions. Some speakers are terrified that someone will interrupt their presentation with a question or comment. Actually, this is one of the best things that can happen: it shows that someone in the audience has engaged with what you're saying, and it can actually lead to genuine progress on the point you were making. And two-way conversation (assuming you're minimally good at it) is always a tension reducer.

15. **Know when to stop lecturing.** Certain presentations—especially in advanced or upper-division classes or seminars—can require you to present some material, then lead a discussion. Be sure to attentively listen to any comments or questions your classmates or professor might raise, before starting on your answer. In a discussion period, never lecture (only discuss), and be sure to answer exactly the question asked (not offer up more canned—but irrelevant—material). In many classes, how you discuss is as important as how you present (in some classes, it's even taken into account in the grade).

Running Scared? How to Build Your Confidence

It's easy to feel a lack of confidence at college. Lectures with hundreds of students can make one feel no bigger than a worm. And even smaller classes can make you feel low when it seems like the student in the front row has all the answers—and the professor's telling him or her so. Luckily, like every other skill, confidence can be learned and can be increased over time. Especially if you follow our fifteen practical tips:

✔ **Turn off the little voice.** Everyone has a part of themselves that from time to time whispers defeating messages: "You're not good enough for college," "Everyone here is more qualified than you," "You'll never pass that mondo midterm." But don't listen. Remind yourself that you've accomplished a lot before getting into this college, and that if you didn't have what it takes to succeed, they wouldn't have admitted you.

✔ **Realize you're not alone.** Everyone thinks they're the only one, but a recent study shows that one-third of college students feel inadequate after the very first semester. We can tell you from our own firsthand experience that a majority of students have doubts at one time or another about their ability to do the work. So if you're feeling unsure of yourself, keep in mind that you're in distinguished company: most of your friends are going through (or have gone through) just what you're experiencing now.

✔ **Take something you're good at.** Each semester, in spite of the distribution requirements and courses you need for your major, take at least one course you enjoy—and are guaranteed to do well in. Constantly struggling at courses that are very, very challenging saps your strength and can, over time, undermine your confidence.

✔ **Start small.** Try taking a few small risks to help you overcome some of your fears. Maybe you could ask (or answer) a question in discussion section. Or approach a professor with a question before or after class. Once you've broken the ice, even a little, you'll begin to feel more secure.

 EXTRA POINTER. Low-risk activities that are built right into the course provide an excellent opportunity to bolster your confidence. Getting a check-plus on a short homework assignment or a ten on the weekly quiz can do wonders for your self-esteem.

✔ **Reward achievements.** Everyone feels better when they give themselves some recognition for a job well done—even a small accomplishment. Get yourself a slice of pizza—with extras—for that ten on the quiz. The positive reinforcement will make it easier for you to study for next week's quiz. And the $2 investment will remind you that your achievements, too, are something worth celebrating.

✔ **Make all the classes.** It's hard to feel confident about yourself when you're missing key pieces of the course—pieces that, when missed, prevent you from doing well and, hence, feeling confident. Students who pop into class erratically have much greater trouble understanding and following the lectures they do attend. And they have much more trouble answering questions on tests that depend on material in classes they missed.

✔ **Take a small class.** Even though it might seem less scary to hide in the anonymity of a huge lecture hall, taking a small class can offer a more supportive and nurturing environment for learning. Especially if you strut your stuff by asking or answering a question and receive positive feedback.

✔ **Get feedback early.** Your confidence can soar if you consult with your professor (or TA) early in the semester. Whether it's about a point in the lecture you didn't understand, your initial ideas for a paper or worries about how to prepare for a test, you will feel immeasurably better after you instructor steers you in the right direction—or assures you that you're already going in the right direction. Many unconfident students are too scared to talk to their professors. This only makes their problem worse. (For more on seeking out your professor, see the "The 15 Secrets of Going to See the Professor" on pp. 129–133.)

✔ **Divide big tasks into small pieces.** Many students doubt their ability to write a fifteen-page research paper or prepare for a comprehensive final. But if they conceived of the paper as three five-page pieces, and the final as five three-week units, the task would suddenly seem a lot more doable. And the feeling of accomplishment generated when one part of the project is completed would help propel them to finish the rest of the work.

✔ **Do a trial run.** Many college projects allow you to do a no-risk practice round before the real thing. Taking a practice test at home before the midterm, trying out your oral presentation on the TA before the section meeting, discussing answers to the study guide with your study group before the final—all of these are things that will build your confidence before the actual event. And if your cohorts or instructor say a few kind words about your ideas—and if you believe they mean them—well, that can help, too.

✔ **Take comments constructively.** Many students see every mark on their paper as a biting criticism and get all depressed or ignore them completely. Train yourself to view the comments in a more positive light, as ways the professor is trying to help you do better on the next piece of work (rather than sink your ship). Learning how to use the comments to improve—even after a not-so-impressive start—can be the best confidence booster of all.

✔ **Apply for a prize.** Many departments have various prize competitions for their majors or for all students at the college. And lots of times the competition isn't as tough as you might think. So give it a whirl. Winning even a $10 gift certificate or a mention on the plaque in the department office can be a real confidence booster.

✔ **Look for real-world apps.** A chance to work at an inner-city clinic (if you're in a health care field), at an engineering consultant firm (if you're interested in waste-management systems), or even in an insurance office (if you're studying marketing) can give you a real shot in the arm. Seeing how what you've learned in college can have real worth in the real world will build your confidence like nothing else. And then, when you return to college next fall, those dull, dreary lectures won't seem quite so meaningless.

✔ **Recognize that learning is a process.** If you expect to master a new field right off the bat, or be able to write a bang-up research paper when you've never written one before, you set yourself up for a letdown—and for a crisis of confidence. Be patient with yourself as you start on new tasks or skills. Think back on skills you mastered in the past (whether it's snowboarding, Texas hold 'em, or vegan cooking) and remember what it was like when you first started.

✔ **Avoid the bubble bursters.** You know who we mean: the people who, no matter how good your achievement, can always find something wrong. For some students, it's their parents; for others, it's their perfectionist professor or adviser; and for still others, it's the person who shares their loft with them. Adopt a "don't ask, don't tell" policy toward such naysayers: they won't ask how you're doing, you won't tell them about your successes.

4

FORCED LABOR

It's unavoidable. Virtually every college has some basic requirements that everyone has to take, like it or not. Might have the name general education, core, distribution, or lower-division requirements. But whatever you call them, you gotta take them. Think of them as having to eat your vegetables or take your medicine.

Colleges are requiring this stuff because it really is good for you (or so they think). So what's not to like here? Well, the problem is that some students get so tied up in these must-do courses—getting C's and D's or, worse, failing them, then having to retake them umpteen times—that what was supposed to be a basic skills-developing or area-exposing course turns into a major GPA-buster and impediment to finishing your degree in a finite number of years.

To smooth your way through the gamut of required courses your school might offer—that is, inflict upon—you, we offer some tips that will help you easily manage the most common, and, for some, the most vex-ing, required courses.

In this chapter, you'll learn:

- ▶ 10 Ways to Whip the Freshman Comp Requirement

- ▶ 10 Tips for Taming the Math Requirement

- ▶ Top 10 Tips for Mastering the Foreign Language Requirement

- ▶ 10 Ideas for Learning to Love the Lab

- ▶ 10 Tips for the First-Year Experience Course

- ▶ How to Take Courses on the 'Net—for Free

10 Ways to Whip the Freshman Comp Requirement

Many students starting college encounter something like this:

ENGL 1013 Composition I (Sp, Su, Fa). Required of all freshmen unless exempted by the Department of English. *Prerequisite:* ENGL 0003 or an acceptable score on the English section of the SAT, ACT, or another approved test.

It's that most despised of all college courses, the freshman composition requirement. A one-size-fits-all course designed to teach you, as they say, "writing across the curriculum"—which in ordinary language means the basics of spelling, grammar, and composition that, ideally, you'll be able to carry over to all your other courses. Skeptical? Who cares? You're stuck. Might as well equip yourself with the ten best tips from Raina Smith Lyons, assistant director of the program in composition at the University of Arkansas:

1. **Go to class.** Sure, you might think that not much goes on in class. And maybe at your high school or even in your other college courses, it's true. But in freshman comp, a majority of the activities are centered around the class meetings. You might have one-on-one critiques of your papers, "workshopping" (that is, peer discussion of rough drafts), presentation of sources that go beyond the textbook, as well as actual in-class writing. And most instructors take roll and count it toward your grade. Upshot? In freshman comp, in particular, it's best to get your a** to class. Every time.

BEST-KEPT SECRET. Many colleges are experimenting with teaching their freshman writing classes online—not because the faculty wants it this way, but because the administration sees it as a way to save money. According to one recent study, at some schools 15 to 25 percent of freshman comp courses have no in-class component. But what they don't tell you is that some of the more valuable course components have been dropped: student presentations, individual conferences with the instructor, and group writing projects have all but disappeared in the virtual course world. Suggestion: if you have a choice between (a) face-to-face and (b) device-to-device, choose (a)—the one with the living, breathing instructor (and live classmates, too).

2. **Do all the work assigned.** Most freshman comp classes have a graduated series of tasks. You start slow, perhaps just by presenting someone's argument, then build up to harder tasks as the semester progresses—such as comparing a number of positions, learning to evaluate the argument, and, ultimately, presenting your own reasoned views. Miss a key step or skill, and you're behind for future work.

EXTRA POINTER. Do all the work, even if it doesn't make sense to you. Some instructors assign "free writing" or other assignments just to get the juices flowing and to motivate you to write more.

3. **Talk to your teacher.** Use e-mail, office hours, or a simple face-to-face conversation after class to make the teacher aware of any problems you're having, like not understanding the assignment, trouble getting started, inability to "prewrite," or wanting to hand in a late assignment. Whatever the case, your instructor is happy to help—if you come to him or her while there is still time.

4. **Finish your drafts early.** One of the main things they're trying to teach in these freshman comp courses is the importance of writing drafts of your work and thinking through the issues over a period of time. This process is thwarted when you leave the draft to the last minute—especially if the teacher has given you three or four weeks to do the essay.

 5-STAR TIP. Program yourself to think the paper is due one week before it really is. That way, you'll have a full week left to do a series of revisions.

5. **Be sure you understand the assignment.** Freshman comp courses often try to teach you to write a general persuasive or critical essay, not to use the tools from any particular discipline or major. So they often teach a variety of kinds of papers, each with its own characteristic structure and tasks. Make sure that for each of the four or five paper assignments you know exactly what's being asked. If the instructor has gone over an outline in class, as many do, be sure to follow it in your paper.

6. **Offer up a good thesis.** Part of the success of a freshman comp paper is determined by the quality of the thesis: the single sentence, usually at the beginning of the paper, that expresses the one key point you're trying to get across in the paper. Pick too obvious or simplistic a thesis, and your paper is heading for a C. Pick a better or deeper thesis, and your paper is on the express track to an A. If you're not sure what your thesis should be, it's well worth your while to run it by the teacher.

7. **Be sure to prove what you've claimed.** In some of the freshman comp assignments you're asked not only to compare or contrast points of view but to provide reasons or arguments for a given claim (whether that of some author or your own). Be sure to do so, if asked.

8. **Go beyond your conclusion.** Usually freshman comp papers ask you to conclude by summing up what you've shown. A really good ending, though, can also go beyond what's been shown in the paper:

either pointing out some further dimension of the issue or offering some broader assessment of your results. Sure, a conclusion is meant to point back. But it can also point forward.

9. **Imaginatively use campus resources.** The writing center, in which you can receive up to an hour's worth of individualized help from a trained writing expert (often an English graduate student), can beat the ten or fifteen minutes you might get from a TA or lecturer. The reference librarian can help you use electronic databases that'll provide strong sources for your paper, if sources are needed. (See "16 Techniques for Doing Research Like a Professor" on pp. 118–122 for more on this.) And did you know that your campus has experts in the faculty of many departments? Your paper "What effects do media have on young children?" could be strengthened by a chat with a professor of cognitive science or child development who actually does research on living, breathing children.

10. **Present good-looking work.** Be sure to proofread your paper manually after you've run the electronic spell-check. Many times there's a homonym, or simply a wrong word, that a spell-checker doesn't catch. Also be sure to take out any sentences that don't do any work or that aren't directly relevant to the task asked: in other words, put yourself in the place of the reader and trim out any fluff. In a composition course, the presentation of the ideas can be as important as the ideas themselves.

BONUS TIP. Play to your interests. You'll enjoy your required freshman comp course more, if, when given a choice, you pick topics that get you excited.

10 Tips for Taming the Math Requirement

For many college students, the math requirement is the single biggest obstacle standing between them and their cap and gown. Believe it or not, some students take the same math course two or three times, and by the end of their ordeal have just barely passed. It doesn't have to be this way. College math is easily manageable, and might even turn out to be fun, if you follow our ten-step plan for acing the math requirement:

1. **Get in—and stay in—the right level.** Colleges often have several levels of calculus and up to five versions of algebra. Select carefully to avoid taking classes that are too hard (or too easy) for your level of ability and training. Double-check after the first test, and switch classes if necessary. Why torture yourself if you're never going to able to master delta-epsilon proofs?

2. **Take the credit.** If you have AP math credits, use 'em. Your first-year adviser or a representative from the math department can tell you what college credit(s) you've earned and what course you should enroll in if you want to continue your study of math.

 BEST-KEPT SECRET. Be sure to figure out whether you've taken the Calculus AB or the Calculus BC course. And if you're lucky enough to have taken the new Statistics AP course, be sure to put in a claim for that, too.

3. **Do every single homework problem.** In other subjects, homework may not be so critical: if you do it, that's great, and if you blow it off, well, that's OK, too (you'll do some extra cramming come test time). But in math it's supercritical to keep up with the homework. Doing the homework problems is the way you learn math. Not to mention the way you learn how to do the various kinds of problems that will

be on the tests. And you'll understand the lecture better if you do the problems when they're assigned.

4. **Always have a strategy.** Never go at math problems with a sledge-hammer. Start by figuring out what type of problem you're dealing with, and consider various strategies for solving this sort of problem. Then select the strategy you think most appropriate or promising. Never lunge wildly with a strategy that's totally inappropriate for the task at hand. You can waste tremendous amounts of time going down blind alleys if you don't think before you do.

5. **Be ultraneat.** In all your math work—whether your class notes, homework, or tests—be obsessive about neatness. A 5 that looks like a 6, an x that looks like a z, or a + that looks like a – will mess you up like you wouldn't believe.

6. **Get down the intermediate steps.** Some instructors are careful to write down every step of a problem as they are doing it in class; other professors (like the ones who are teaching this course for the hundred and eighth time) aren't so fastidious. In either case, you should be sure to write down what the professor puts up, then when you get home, fill in whatever steps have been omitted (if any).

IOHO. Many students complain that they can't understand what their non-native-English-speaking TA is saying. Many of these complaints are unfounded. But if you really can't understand your TA or professor's English, we recommend you go to an office hour and engage him or her in basic conversation (not techni-cal math talk). Often, once you've had an ordinary conversation, you'll get used to your teacher's accent, which will make the classes go a whole lot easier. But if after all that you still can't understand your TA's English, change to another section. You can't learn if you can't understand.

7. **Pinpoint your sticking points.** When you get stuck on a problem, don't just throw up your hands in disgust and announce you're clue-less. Figure out exactly where you got stuck—and for what reason

(Was there a theorem you didn't know? Were you missing a concept? Did you fail to consider an alternative?). Then go for help. The help will be much more effective, and the helper more motivated to give it, if you can locate your exact problem, rather than just reporting your veil of confusion. (For some tips on seeking help, see "The 15 Secrets of Going to See the Professor" on pp. 129–133.)

8. **Join a group.** Study groups (once or twice a week) are especially valuable in problem-solving courses like math. Even if you're a math whiz, you can benefit from teaching your less gifted friends how to do the problems or proofs. Making challenging material clear to others is one of the best ways of getting your mind around difficult concepts and strategies.

EXTRA POINTER. If your TA is holding a group office hour or review session before a test, make it your business to go. When the TA has the test questions in mind, he or she is most likely to drop hints about what's going to be asked.

9. **Test yourself.** By far the best way to study for math tests is to prepare a test for yourself and do the problems. You'll see very quickly what you know—and what you don't.

5-STAR TIP. Most textbooks have extra problems in the back, with answers provided for at least half of them, usually the odd-numbered ones. These make great choices for your practice tests. Also, some professors give out sample problems or copies of previous tests before the exam: don't squander this important resource by taking "just a quick peek" at the questions as you put the handout into your backpack. And, if all else fails, make up your own problems: construct variants, preferably harder variants, of the ones you did in class or on the homework.

10. **Think about tutoring.** If you're really having difficulty in your math class, you might want to find a tutor. Sometimes a TA who has previously taught the course is available, sometimes an upperclassperson can help you out, and sometimes the on-campus learning center or math lab has trained people available to help you. Just make sure the tutor is both good at math and familiar with the particular course (and, in the best case, the instructor) you're taking. And be sure to bring the textbook, your class notes, the problems you've done, and, most important, any info about the tests, to each of the meetings with your tutor. That way, he or she can tailor the tutoring sessions to your exact needs.

 BONUS TIP. Adopt a can-do attitude. Don't let some label your third-grade teacher put on you rule your life today. If you tell yourself "I'm just not good at math," or "I'm intuitive, not logical," or "girls just can't do math as well as boys," you've defeated yourself even before you start. Why do that?

Top 10 Tips for Mastering the Foreign Language Requirement

Fala português? Puhutko suomea? Sen söyle türk? Spreekt u nederlands? Kana (or Kina, as the case may be) Hausa? All of these are ways of asking whether you speak some language: Portuguese, Finnish, Turkish, Dutch, and Hausa, respectively. You, too, would know this, if you had completed your foreign language requirement in one of these tongues. Or at least you'd know what *¿Habla usted español?* or *Parlez-vous français?* mean (not telling you these).

To help you get through your foreign language requirement—a four-course sequence at most four-year colleges—here are our ten best strategies:

1. **Pick for a reason.** The foreign language requirement is one of the very few two-year requirements at many colleges. Select your language for a reason. Good reason: Pashto will be useful in your career at the State Department. Less good reason: I took Spanish in high school and kinda, sorta—well, now that I think of it—didn't really like all that much.

2. **Attend all the classes.** The foreign language class is one of the few classes that is truly cumulative: every lesson includes some content that, together with the other classes, builds your knowledge of the language. Your usual "cutting allowance" won't cut it in foreign languages.

3. **Learn the conjugations—both ways.** The secret to learning languages is mastering the verbs, not the nouns. So practice the verb conjugations (you know: *I am, you are, he is...*) in both directions—that is, from the foreign language into English and from English into the foreign language. In some courses, the tests could ask you to go both ways. And even if that's not required, you'll learn the forms really well only if you practice both ways (flash cards, especially

the new electronic flash cards put out by WWW.STUDYBLUE.COM, are especially helpful here).

4. **Learn all the "moods."** No, not your moods (you know those already), but the verb moods. Subjunctive, conditional, aorist—each language has its own (Czech reportedly has ten tenses, voices, moods, and aspects). As you move past the first year in your study of the language, these unusual-to-English-speaker moods become increasingly important.

5. **Pay attention to sentence structure.** Though English usually is arranged in subject-verb-predicate order, many other languages don't follow this pattern. Master the way your new language structures and constructs the sentence—to the point that you can anticipate what's coming next as the sentence unfolds (which will help get you away from word-by-word translation or sentence construction—an achievement in itself).

6. **Learn how it sounds.** Americans are really bad at vowels. But foreign languages often have many grades of vowels and many vowels that sound different from English. Learn the proper pronunciation—and the length—of vowels.

7. **Memorize in bite-size pieces.** Every language requires memorizing vocabulary. You'll have a much easier time if you memorize a few words each day, rather than leave 484 words 'til the midterm.

8. **Beware of "false friends."** In every language there are words that sound a lot like an English word, but mean something else entirely. For example, in virtually every language but English, a "preservative" is something you might need on a romantic date but wouldn't want to find in your peanut butter. Check out this false friend and gazillions of others at HTTP://EN.WIKIPEDIA.ORG/WIKI/FALSE_FRIENDS.

9. **"Friend" a foreign student.** The only really good way to learn a language is by talking with a native speaker. So find an international friend and have ordinary conversations with him or her. That way, you'll learn not only the language in context but also all the words

you really need to know (but somehow never learned in Portuguese 102). Failing that, try going to a language lab or language table to practice your conversation.

BEST-KEPT SECRET.　There are many opportunities on the Web to practice your language with native speakers in exotic locales. These include WWW.LIVEMOCHA.COM, at which you can chat for free with over a million native speakers in twelve languages. (What a deal—foreign language plus social networking!) And for students who'd like to subscribe (and pay a small monthly fee), check out WWW.CHINESEPOD.COM (and its sister sites WWW.FRENCHPOD.COM, WWW.SPANISHPOD.COM, and WWW.ITALIANPOD.COM): you'll find over a thousand podcasts, along with practice, review, and reinforcement. Another very good site (recommended by one of our students) is WWW.RADIOLINGUA.COM: here you'll find the very popular CoffeeBreakSpanish and CoffeeBreakFrench podcasts, as well as the One-Minute podcasts in, among other languages, Irish, Polish, Russian, and even Luxembourgish.

5-STAR TIP.　It's always fun to listen to the evening news in the language you're studying (you'll learn interesting things about the culture, too). Check out your TV, the Web, YouTube, or other content areas for broadcasts and recordings. If you're studying Spanish, check out the new Spanish Immersion TV site at HTTP://LOMASTV.COM.

10. **Entertain your prof (or TA) in the language.** If you visit your teacher in an office hour, or talk with him or her after class, be sure to converse in the foreign language. That'll not only give you some spontaneous practice in talking the stuff, but earn you some brownie points for trying really hard.

BONUS TIP. Make peace with your lot. For better or worse, many schools require four courses in one foreign language. Try to do well in them, and don't fall behind. Most of all, stick with the one you start. We've seen countless students take a semester of French, switch to German, only to try Italian. False starts in foreign languages are one of the main reasons college can drag on for more than four years.

10 Ideas for Learning to Love the Lab

Many schools have a lab requirement. And many students hate the lab requirement almost as much as they hate the freshman comp, math, and foreign language requirements. Too boring, too hard, too stupid: these are common complaints students have. But it doesn't have to be this way. Especially if you follow our ten best tips for conquering the lab requirement:

1. **Know what you're picking.** At many schools, there's a broad variety of courses that satisfy the lab requirement. You might be surprised to know that in addition to "hard" sciences such as chemistry, physics, and biology, in many schools astronomy, geology, anthropology, environmental science, and psychology can count toward the lab requirement. Suggestion: pick something that you like and that you wouldn't ordinarily have a chance to take. This is one of your best opportunities at college to turn a requirement into an elective—something you *choose* to take because you like it.

2. **Know which courses count for a science major.** Sometimes you'll want to take a course that will both satisfy the distribution requirement and count toward a major. Be sure in such a case that the course you select will in fact do double duty. Some courses—for example, physics for humanities majors or the biology of everyday life—are specifically excluded from the major. They're geared to the general university population and, hence, too easy for serious scientists (or even majors).

 EXTRA POINTER. Be sure to figure out when your lab meets. An astronomy course could involve night trips to the observatory, while an earth sciences course might go out on field trips to look at rock formations.

3. **Attend to the "requisites."** Some lab courses, especially ones that can count for the major, have prerequisites and/or corequisites: courses you have to have completed before—or at the same time as—the lab you're taking. Especially important in physics, chemistry, and sometimes biology is the amount of math that's required. Some courses are algebra-based (or, in street language, presuppose high school math), while others are nonalgebra-based (that is, require calculus and often involve a good amount of theory).

EXTRA POINTER. Often the course description isn't fully explicit about the prerequisites, or the professor is implicitly assuming some level of math training. If in doubt, ask.

4. **Take it on time.** It's always good to polish off the lab requirement in one of your first two years of college. And if the information from the courses is needed for some upcoming professional exam—the MCAT, DAT, GRE, or GMAT, for instance—it's an especially good idea not to run this requirement down to the wire.

5-STAR TIP. You'll want to take the lab in the same semester as you're taking the lecture. You wouldn't believe it, but some students take the course, and leave the (unpleasant-for-them) lab to another semester (by which time they've forgotten all the material).

5. **Do the pre- and post-work.** Many lab courses have an in-class and an out-of-class component. In advance of the lab, you might be asked to read the lab manual and write out answers to some questions; after some labs, you might have to write up a two- to three-page lab report summing up your methods, reporting your results, and drawing some conclusions. Be sure to do all this assigned work. It'll help you understand the lectures in the courses, the

demonstrations in the lab, and, in some courses, will count toward the grade and could even appear on the tests. Why row with only one oar in the water?

6. **Connect it.** Many students consider the lab as a self-contained activity, not as something connected to other parts of the course. (This view is reinforced by the fact that at many schools you sign up for a one-credit lab course under a different number than the science lecture itself.) You'll understand the lab better if you ask yourself, *How is this lab supposed to reinforce the concepts of the course? Why is it placed at the point in the course it is? Why are you doing a lab at all?* (Possible answer: *the last lecture drew ray diagrams, and this lab shows the real, physical properties that rays exhibit in different media.*)

7. **Volunteer for demos.** Many labs include a portion where the professor (or TA) calls for volunteers to assist in some demonstration. Be the guinea pig. Not only will you enjoy showing off your erudition to your classmates (and to the professor), you might actually enjoy doing the stuff. And if you do a really good job in the demonstration—like answering the questions with the key concepts from the class—you might get a few extra points when the prof calculates the grade.

8. **Play all the parts.** In many labs, the students are divided into groups of three or four, with various tasks assigned to each. There could be the "Do-er," the "Recorder," the "Time-Manager," and the "Question Asker" (YRMV, depending on the lab). Take your turn in each of the roles. Not only will it make the lab more interesting, you'll learn (and remember) the material better if sometimes you're actually mixing the chemicals, dissecting the amoeba, or rolling the ball down the plane—not just taking the notes, watching the stopwatch, or asking some superobvious question.

9. **Think abstractly.** It's an important part of every lab to observe the experiment and record what you see. But it's also important to apply the theories, principles, and constructs of the course to what you've seen (look to the lectures and readings for these). The professor doesn't only want you to say that the ball started rolling faster as it got to the bottom of the hill, he or she wants you to apply the

concepts of kinetic and potential energy, acceleration, and gravity to the case. (Hey, this isn't your seventh-grade science fair.)

10. **Use the office hours.** It's a good idea to seek out your professor, TA, or lab instructor when writing up the lab report, especially if it counts toward the grade. (If you have a week to write the report, go early in the week.) You'll be able to make sure you've understood the science and captured the key concepts—not just parroted the purpose and procedures of the experiment straight out the lab manual. And be sure to make the corrections that the instructor suggests. Even if it's a pain to go back and fix up the report you thought was finished, you'll get a better result. And who knows? You might actually learn something, if you take the time to learn from an expert. Didn't expect to do that in what you thought was a cruddy distribution requirement, did you?

10 Tips for the First-Year Experience Course

One of the hottest new things at college is the first-year experience (FYE) course—a one-semester class that matches the very best faculty of the school (or, at least, well-trained TAs) with an engaging, often relevant, subject of study. All in a small-group, friendly atmosphere. Some schools focus their first-year experience courses on easing the transition from high school to college: these courses emphasize academic skills, personal development, and learning your way around the campus. Other schools adopt a "professor's prerogative" model: here, professors are invited to teach a course on a topic in which they are doing research—or are just plain interested in thinking about. Under this model—sometimes called a freshman seminar (FS)—you might find courses such as: *Comic Books and Conflict*; *Midwives, Healers, and Physicians*; or *Energy: What We Use and Where It Should Come From* (these courtesy of City University of New York; check your college's online catalogue for the options at your campus).

Whatever kind of first-year course your school offers, you'll want to get off to the best possible start—which you will, if you follow these ten best tips from visiting professor J. Steven Reznick, associate dean for first-year seminars at the University of North Carolina:

1. **Make a list.** Each first-year experience course will be limited to approximately fifteen to twenty-five students, so even at a small school you might not get your first choice of classes. Enrolling in any first-year seminar is better than enrolling in no first-year seminar, so be strategic: look at the first-year seminar offerings at your school and come up with a list of seminars that would be of interest.

 EXTRA POINTER. If you'd like to see what an elaborate FYE program looks like, take a look at UCLA's (WWW.COLLEGE.UCLA.EDU/FIATLUX) or UNC's (WWW.UNC.EDU/FYS).

2. **Play to your strengths.** Some first-year seminars emphasize in-class discussion, while others emphasize hands-on activities, social interactions, creativity, or community service. When putting together your list of seminars, pick a class that is not only on a topic you're interested in, but is built upon a type of activity that you enjoy.

3. **Avoid your major.** Some students enter school with leanings toward a specific major, and think it would be natural to look for seminars in that major. Not generally a good idea. When you get into your major, you'll have lots of advanced courses on interesting topics in that field. Think of your first-year experience course as an opportunity to explore completely new territory: something that just sounds interesting or that you've always wanted to learn about.

4. **Speak up.** If your seminar encourages discussion, open your mouth (even if public speaking makes you a little uncomfortable). A first-year seminar is a great context for you to get beyond your high school timidity and find your college voice.

5. **Add some spice to the stew.** Even if your seminar is not focused on discussion, it is supposed to be interesting, and instructors are always glad to have student participation. You can help by asking questions, introducing new ideas, and steering the course toward interesting topics.

6. **Show up.** Class attendance is always the right thing to do (not only because it is the key to getting a good education, but because you're paying for the classes). But in a first-year seminar—with only fifteen to twenty-five students—your absence from class will really be noticeable. More important, first-year seminars are often an ongoing conversation or debate built on previous presentations and discussions. So if you aren't in class, you aren't in the dialogue.

7. **Keep in mind that first-year experience courses are still courses.** Don't lose sight of the fact that, although your first-year seminar has some qualities that make it different from traditional courses, it's still a regular course that might count as credit hours, might meet your school's gen ed requirements, and might be graded. Have fun in your first-year seminar, but don't forget to get the job done.

8. **Make friends.** One important aspect of first-year seminars is the opportunity to make new friendships. The word "make" is an active verb: sitting back and waiting for friendships to happen is generally not an effective strategy. You can play an active role in helping make friendships happen by starting conversations, issuing invitations, and organizing events.

9. **Build a relationship with your instructor.** If most of your other first-year courses are huge, the instructor in your first-year seminar could be the faculty member you know best and who knows you best. Getting off to a good start with one prof can be helpful in many ways: picking future courses, getting academic advice, and ultimately obtaining a letter of recommendation. Your first-year seminar offers a great opportunity to make this connection.

10. **Spread the word.** Interesting first-year seminar topics can initiate a wave that extends far beyond the classroom. Talk about your seminar with parents, friends, and the stranger sitting beside you on the bus or in the cafeteria. You'll learn more deeply about the focal topic by describing your seminar to others and by thinking about their questions and observations.

How to Take Courses on the 'Net—for Free

Once you've polished off your required coursework (or even before), you might want to take a course because you're actually interested in the subject. Trouble is, not every course is offered at every university—especially if yours is a small college and you have a very specialized interest. Luckily, you live in a very special time. Thanks to the generosity of the William and Flora Hewlett Foundation and the Andrew W. Mellon Foundation—and the work of the OpenCourseWare (OCW) initiative of universities worldwide—you can take any of eight thousand courses at the very best universities online. All without paying a dime, and at the time and place of your choice. Sound too good to be true? Here's how:

1. **Find the sites.** Begin by searching either the master list of all courses provided by the OpenCourseWare Consortium WWW.OCWCONSORTIUM.ORG/USE/USE-DYNAMIC.HTML—or else surf on over to one of the sites of the major participating universities:

    MIT: WWW.OCW.MIT.EDU

    Yale: WWW.OYC.YALE.EDU

    Notre Dame: HTTP://OCW.ND.EDU

    Carnegie Mellon: HTTPS://OLI.WEB.CMU.EDU/OPENLEARNING/ FORSTUDENTS/FREECOURSES

    UC Berkeley: HTTP://WEBCAST.BERKELEY.EDU

    UC Irvine: HTTP://OCW.UCI.EDU

    Tufts: HTTP://OCW.TUFTS.EDU

    Stanford: HTTP://ITUNES.STANFORD.EDU

    Utah State: HTTP://OCW.USU.EDU

BEST-KEPT SECRET. A very useful resource (different from those mentioned above) is WWW.OCWFINDER.COM. Here you can search for courses using a wide variety of filters.

FLASH! A new Web site that describes itself as "a perpetually improving educational ecosystem" gathers some of the best courses from ten leading universities: WWW.ACADEMICEARTH.ORG. Check it out.

2. **Play to their strengths.** Every college has some fields they're strong in and other fields in which they're less distinguished. You won't be surprised to hear that biology, chemistry, physics, statistics and math are strong at MIT and Carnegie Mellon; philosophy, religion, and history, at Yale, Notre Dame, and Berkeley; and biological and irrigation engineering, at Utah State. If you have the skills and knowledge needed, try to take the courses you want at the best schools that offer them.

3. **Take something that interests you.** You'll be more motivated to listen to all the lectures if you pick a subject for which you have a true passion. Some of the ones we liked included:

Donald Kagan's *Introduction to Ancient Greek History* (Yale, Classics)

Shelly Kagan's *Death* (Yale, Philosophy)

Amy Hungerford's *American Novel Since 1945* (Yale, English)

Asma Afsaruddin's *Women in Islamic Societies* (Notre Dame, Middle Eastern Studies)

Norman Crowe's *Nature and the Built Environment* (Notre Dame, Architecture)

Gary Merkley's *Sprinkle and Trickle Irrigation* (Utah State, Biological and Irrigation Engineering)

4. **Pick your modality.** Some of the courses offer full video downloads, others just audio, and still others just print materials. While we're partial to the video lectures—the closest thing to being there in person—students listening to the class on the freeway or the treadmill will prefer the audio classes. Safer, too.

5. **Pick your language.** Some of the courses (especially at the MIT site) offer translations into foreign languages, including Spanish, Portuguese, Chinese (traditional and simplified), Persian, and Thai. So if English is not your native language, you might enjoy the top-notch courses in your native tongue. The OCW Consortium Web site also offers courses at universities in countries ranging from Afghanistan to Vietnam—with special concentrations in France, Iran, Japan, Korea, and Spain.

EXTRA POINTER. Some of the sites even offer closed-captioning—good if you're hearing impaired or if you find it easier to learn with subtitles.

6. **Learn the layout.** Course Web pages are usually arranged in the standard order of the college semester. You'll typically find on the left side of your screen the course description, instructor bio, syllabus, topics and readings for individual lectures, tests and paper assignments, and downloads. On the right side of the screen, look for related resources that often provide a wealth of material for additional study on topics of interest.

7. **Get the readings.** It's always worthwhile to get your hands on the assigned readings and exercises, since they'll make for a richer course experience and better learning.

EXTRA POINTER. If your university library doesn't have the assigned readings, check with the interlibrary loan (ILL) department for help getting them.

8. **Negotiate credit.** If you're planning to do all the work, see if you can get credit for the course as a directed or individual studies course. At some universities—especially if your university doesn't offer the course you're taking, or offers only a lower-level version—you'll be able to sign up with a professor at your own school and get course credit.

 5-STAR TIP. In making your pitch, be sure to mention that you intend to hand in the papers to your resident professor and take the tests under test conditions.

9. **Customize your learning.** Some learners will like to listen only to a portion of the lectures—those on a topic they're especially interested in. Some will like to take an advance peek at the midterm and final, so that they'll know in advance what points the professor thinks are most important. And still others will like to batch lectures together and have an eight-hour marathon of all the lectures on some topic. One of the great advantages of courses on the Web is that you control the speed and intensity of the learning. Make the course fit your learning style.

10. **Make it a community activity.** A few courses offer online communities of fellow students taking the course in cyberspace; if you're lucky enough to have hit on one of these, join the community. If not, you can invite a friend to take a class with you. Then you can set up your own viewings, discussion or study groups, and—if you have multiple friends in the class—a Facebook page for the course.

5

IT'S SHOWTIME!

There are times at college when you have to perform. And not just in some little sideshow, but a major front-and-center performance. We're talking about tests and papers—the two or three or four moments over the course of the semester that really count. These are the times when large chunks of points, or large percentages of the grade, are up for grabs. It's a very rare student indeed who can waltz into the test or approach the due date on the paper without his or her adrenal glands' pumping out some serious cortisol.

Now we can't promise to eliminate every preperformance jitter or butterfly, but we can offer you behind-the-scenes tips and techniques that'll give you more power and confidence come the dreaded test and paper times. This advice can help you keep the lid on your limbic system (for you nonbiology majors, that's the so-called emotional brain) as you face down these big moments of college.

In this chapter you'll learn:

- ▶ 12 Tips for A+ Test Preparation
- ▶ How to Figure Out What's Going to Be on the Test
- ▶ Top 13 Test-Taking Tips
- ▶ 10 Tips for Writing the Perfect Paper
- ▶ Top 10 Ways of Making the Leap from a B to an A
- ▶ 16 Techniques for Doing Research Like a Professor

12 Tips for A+ Test Preparation

It happens every semester. You have to face that much-anticipated test, on which part of this semester's grade now rests. Sorry, we can't make the test or midterm into a walk in the park. Only your professors can—and we wouldn't be counting on that. But how well you prepare will in no small measure determine how well you do. So here are our dozen best test-prep tips (together with a brief glance into the professor's mind to show why they work):

1. **Spend a week.** Start studying for each exam at least a week before you are due to take it. This will give you time to divide the material into manageable portions that you can digest over a number of study sessions. This is especially important in the case of a test with tons of material. Whatever you do, don't try to swallow the whole elephant—the whole course, we mean—in one cram session. (This works because in most courses the prof is expecting you to have processed and digested the material—something you can't do in one fell swoop).

2. **Scope out the scope.** Be sure you know what's fair game on the test and what's not. Many times students aren't exactly sure which lectures, readings, sections, and homework are to be covered on the test. (Does the test include the material that was on the last test? Is the most recent lecture included? Are we responsible for that article discussed in section?) You can't study right if you don't know what you're supposed to be studying. (This works because the prof's assuming you've paid attention when he or she said what's going to be covered on the test.)

3. **Do, don't redo.** Preparing for the test is not the time to reread all the reading, recopy all your notes, or listen to all the lectures again. Time constraints (like the need to keep up with your other work) just don't allow for this. Instead, concentrate on working with the materials you have: the reading and lecture notes and what you can remember

from having heard the lectures once. (This works because you prob-ably remember, or can recover, more than you think. And even if you can't, you simply don't have time to do it from scratch.)

EXTRA POINTER. If you haven't done some key parts of the reading, you need to assess the relative importance of the read-ing versus the lecture notes. Time is of the essence now, and atoning for missed readings by reading them now might not be the best strategy.

4. **Discover the plot.** Now that you're up to the test, you are in a posi-tion to know how the parts of the course up to that point fit together and what all those highfalutin' statements about course objectives on the syllabus really meant. Use this understanding to guide your studying for the exam. (This works because in most courses the main plot of the course is what the professor wants you to have learned and, therefore, what he or she will ask you about on the exam.)

5. **Figure out the format.** There are many kinds of questions your pro-fessor could be asking—multiple choice, short answer, essay, prob-lem solving. Make sure you know which is his or her favorite type of question. (This works because you study better when you know what kind of test you're studying for.) For more tips on anticipating what kinds of questions you're likely to encounter, see "So What's Going to Be on the Test Anyway?" on pp. 105–107.

6. **Mark up your class notes.** The time for obsessively neat notes is now officially over. Go ahead and mark up your notes—both class notes and, if you have them, reading notes. Highlight the main points or draw arrows or stars at central issues. Make notes in the margins about how the main points interrelate. (This works because forcing yourself to actively process your notes helps you locate the key con-cepts and their interrelation—just what the prof is going to be asking about on the test.)

5-STAR TIP. If you don't have a full set of notes for the class, it'd behoove you to ask someone in your class (preferably someone smarter than you) to borrow his or her notes. And if you've taken notes on scraps of paper or scattered pages, it wouldn't be a half-bad idea to arrange the pages in lecture order either. You'd be amazed how many students can't find the plot of the course or locate relations between points simply because their notes are out of order.

7. Load up your mind. Some classes require that you memorize a certain body of material. Perhaps it's verb conjugations in a German class, theorems in a logic class, or the dates of particular events in U.S. history. Take the time to do this drudgework. (This works because sometimes you'll get many points simply for spitting it all back. And even if just storing the content in your mind isn't directly rewarded, the exam could ask you to perform higher-level tasks that require you to have memorized the items—for example, a translation exercise that requires recognizing the verb forms or a math proof that requires application of a theorem.)

 EXTRA POINTER. Use acronyms—words formed from the initial letters of the things to be memorized. Make them as clever as you can (they're easier to remember that way), and then sing them out loud while making faces and flapping your arms (you'll remember the tunes and your bizarro motions).

8. Capture the concepts. In many courses, the real studying work is to get your mind around the key concepts and central ideas of the course. This isn't just memorizing some code words (as in the previous tip), but really understanding the main points. (This works because in an essay exam, what's being graded isn't so much your recall of key points, but your ability to explain them clearly enough, and in enough detail, to communicate a real understanding of the idea.)

9. **Construct a pretest.** Before the test, take matters into your own hands and make up your own exam with questions of the same format as you'll see on the test. Then try out your test under "test conditions": writing it out, timing for each part, no breaks, and no peeking at the book or your notes. (This works because if you pretest, you'll know what to expect and have had some practice doing it.)

 5-STAR TIP. Be sure to monitor—and evaluate—your test-taking performance as you go. If you find that you're devoting too much time to one question, or spending too much time thinking rather than writing, or getting so tensed up that you can hardly think straight, make a mental note. Then when you've finished your trial run, think up strategies you can employ so you can avoid the same pitfalls when you take the real test.

10. **Go to office hours.** It's always worthwhile asking the prof (or TA) if he or she will go over the test you've constructed. Ask whether your answers were good ones and whether your questions were the kinds of questions that could come up on the test. (This works because you'll be getting one-to-one, directed feedback on your work, and, with any luck, the prof or TA might drop some hints about what's going to be on the actual test.)

11. **Make the review session.** If your prof or TA is holding a review session the night before the test (which sometimes happens in large courses, often before the midterm and/or final)—well, that's a gift from God. Most likely they'll "go over" the course material to date and emphasize the important points. (This works because this is the time when professors are especially eager to help the students, so they give particularly useful information. And since they've often just made up the exam, or are planning to write it that night, they can't help dropping some serious hints about what's going to be on the test.)

12. **Observe the "eight-hour rule."** Stop studying for your exam at least eight hours before it begins. The idea here is to keep you from walking into your exam like a zombie from lack of sleep (or all wired up

on Red Bull, Adderall, or who knows what). This eight-hour rule also allows time for the ideas and concepts you've studied to settle into your brain. Trust us. It's been scientifically proven that people who study right up to the last minute perform worse than those who have had a period of relaxation prior to the test. (This works because of a simple equation: lucid, clear thinking = lucid, clear writing = lucid, clear grades.)

 BONUS TIP. The morning of the exam, have an Egg McMuffin or at least a cholesterol-free egg and reduced-fat white cheddar breakfast sandwich. Your brain will work better with carbs and protein (even in reduced dosages). And while you're at it, don't forget to take out a double espresso for the test. Hey, you've studied like a fiend. Why not load up like a fiend?

"So What's Going to Be on the Test Anyway?"

For some college students, nothing will match that moment of terror when they look down at their test and find questions they've never thought of staring back at them. But at that very same moment there's usually some student somewhere else in the room feeling smug satisfaction at having sussed out the exact questions in advance. (Lynn even admits to once wasting valuable exam time shooting "I told you so" looks at her BFF and study partner.) How can you figure out in advance what's going to be on the test—and dramatically increase your chances of acing that exam? Here are some clues from behind the curtain:

☛ **Clue #1:** **Professors test what they talk.** Students often think professors are out to trick them by testing picky, obscure issues. Nothing can be farther from the truth. Professors usually try to teach the most important material—and then test it to see if students have mastered it. Kind of makes sense once you think about it, doesn't it? So look over your notes and see what the prof spent the most time on. That's likely to provide the most fodder for the test.

☛ **Clue #2:** **Professors ask what interests them.** In many courses, you can detect some issue that really excites the prof so much that he or she brings it up again and again, even as the course moves from topic to topic. It's a good bet that your prof's obsession will pop up on the test in some form or other.

☛ **Clue #3:** **Professors drop hints.** Much as we try to keep mum, most professors can't help themselves. They have high-value information that throngs of adulating students are eager to get—and that they are eager to give. So take seriously comments like, "Wow, this would make a really good test question" or "and speaking of...(nudge, nudge, wink, wink)." It might all sound like a joke, but it's not.

☛ Clue #4:   **TAs spill the beans even more than professors.** TAs are usually younger and less experienced. And would like to be liked. So they'll usually cave quickly if you ask them a few questions after class or in office hours—or just show up to section meeting. No bribery necessary!

> **EXTRA POINTER.** Be sure to write down in your notes—ideally, word for word—any hints your prof or TA drops in lecture, discussion, an office hour, or a review session. Come study time, these hints, including their exact phraseology, can prove gold mines of information for what will be on the test.

☛ Clue #5:   **Professors are lazy.** Professors are pretty busy and don't have much time to write entirely new exams. With the result that many times profs will simply reuse—or modify slightly—questions they asked last time around. If you can dig up one of the old exams from a friend who took the same course, from library reserves, from fraternity or sorority files, or (if your stars are aligned) from the prof him- or herself, you can get a pretty good idea of what to expect.

> **5-STAR TIP.** Be sure not to use Dr. O's exam to study for Professor P's upcoming test—even if both teach the same course. Most likely Professor P thinks Dr. O is a loser and would never be caught dead asking such idiotic questions.

☛ Clue #6:   **Professors tell it up front.** The syllabus often lists the educational goals of the course, which can give pretty good valuable information about the test questions. After the first day of class, you might never cast another glance at the syllabus, but it can actually give clues about what the professor thinks is most important—and what he or she's likely to want to test you on. The same applies to the titles for individual lectures or the questions for study for each meeting (if any).

☞ **Clue #7:** **Professors recycle.** Not only questions from previous years, but questions or problems from the homework, quizzes, and problem sets often reappear in slightly different form on the test. Hey, everybody's going green these days.

 5-STAR TIP. If the professor hands out a study guide or "sample" questions—well, that's a no-brainer. Those kinds of questions—or sometimes those very questions—are bound to appear on the test.

Top 13 Test-Taking Tips

Many college students shudder at the thought of the first test—or any test. You shouldn't. Especially if you follow our baker's dozen of best tips for acing the exam:

1. **Bring a beverage.** A nice drink enables you to relax and concentrate on the task at hand. You might even be able to trick yourself into thinking that the next fifty minutes will be a productive and satisfying work hour. At least you won't be thirsty.

2. **Survey the landscape.** When you first get the test, look over the whole thing. Figure out what the tasks are, paying special attention to how many questions you're supposed to answer (be sure to note any choices offered). You'd be amazed at how many students make mistakes about the basic instructions.

3. **Budget your time.** Make a plan for how much time you're going to spend on each question (some professors tell you, in which case you should make sure to follow their instructions). Be sure to devote the most time to the parts of the exam that net the most points— not the ones you like best or know most about. Spending tons of time on questions that don't count much is neither cost- nor grade-effective.

4. **Don't waste time.** Some students begin their exam by writing elaborate outlines or reproducing long lists they've memorized. Don't. If you need to jot down a few notes or a couple of acronyms, that's fine, but you need to spend most of your time writing out the answer, not preparing to write it.

EXTRA POINTER. Another major time waster in cases where a professor offers a choice of topics is to get far into an essay, only to stop and choose another question. It's not uncommon for a professor to find a page—or even several pages—crossed off, followed by an essay on another topic that the student didn't have time to finish. Ouch.

 REALITY CHECK. It's never a good idea to answer all the choices on the theory that the prof will read them all, then give you the grade for the best one. The prof, who has about five minutes (or ten minutes at most) to read your exam, will just read the first choice. No prof is going to do triple the work for your indecisiveness—or your attempt to game the system.

5. **Consider the alternatives.** On a multiple-choice test, make sure you've read all the choices before deciding on one answer. Sometimes the correct answer lies in making a small differentiation between a number of very similar answers. And, of course, unless they're taking off points for wrong answers (which professors almost never do), always fill in something (even if it's all e's.)

 EXTRA POINTER. Forget all the high school tricks, like favoring d's and e's (because "the teacher wants you to read all the choices"); never picking answers with the words *all* or *none* ("things are never as categorical as that"); or always varying your choices ("no teacher would pick three c's in a row"). These strategies are unlikely to work at college. Professors haven't been to high school in a long time. And no one has bothered to remind them of these practices.

6. **Size can matter.** When confronting a short-answer question, consider the possibility of writing two or three or four sentences, rather than just a few code words. What seems "short" to you might seem microscopic to the professor and not be enough to show your understanding of the issue. Also, in a problem-focused test, be sure to show all your work. Even if you don't get the correct answer, the grader might see that you were on the right track and give you partial credit.

7. **Answer exactly the question asked.** Believe it or not, more points are lost on essay tests by not answering precisely the question asked than by giving wrong answers. Professors devote lots of time to constructing their questions, so you can assume they really mean what they ask.

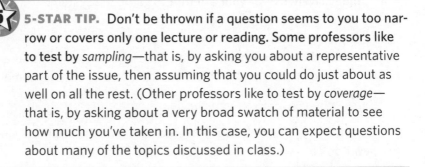

5-STAR TIP. Don't be thrown if a question seems to you too narrow or covers only one lecture or reading. Some professors like to test by *sampling*—that is, by asking you about a representative part of the issue, then assuming that you could do just about as well on all the rest. (Other professors like to test by *coverage*— that is, by asking about a very broad swatch of material to see how much you've taken in. In this case, you can expect questions about many of the topics discussed in class.)

8. **Explain, don't gesture.** Some students think the answer is so obvious—and the professor knows it, after all—that they only need to wave their hands at the answer (rather than wasting all that ink to spell it out). But the prof is looking for you to demonstrate your knowledge and understanding of the material, which can only be done if you take the time to make explicit your points. Be sure your answers can be understood by a reasonably intelligent person— not only one who is previously familiar with the material (like the professor).

9. **Be specific.** Be sure to bring in examples and illustrations to bolster the points you make. Ideas are much more clear when they're

illustrated, not just presented. And be sure to consider all elements of the course—not just the lectures, but also the assigned readings, the discussion sections (if any), and any out-of-class activities—for possible sources of examples. Some ingenuity here can really strengthen your answer—and impress the professor in the process.

10. **Keep it real.** Write in simple, clear language. You're not going to impress the professor when you use all sorts of words whose meanings you don't really know, or lard your paper with all sorts of jargon that you feel you somehow must get in. And avoid BS or other sorts of fillers, and any irrelevant material. When an instructor is reading seventy essays on the same topic, extra junk that is unrelated to the topic really stands out like a sore thumb. Some graders just ignore it, but others will take off points.

11. **Give 'em a break.** Take pity on your grader, who is facing a huge stack of exams and would prefer scrubbing toilet bowls to wading through the pile. Begin to give your answer in the very first sentence (except if you're specifically instructed otherwise) so your grader doesn't have to excavate to unearth it. Number the question you're answering and label any parts. Divide your essay into paragraphs. Circle your answer to a math or science problem. Don't have arrows pointing to who-knows-what page. And it wouldn't hurt if someone could actually read your writing. A happier grader makes for a happier grade.

12. **Keep your cool.** Some questions are meant to be hard. That's how the prof separates the sheep (who get the A's) from the goats (who get the B's). Don't panic if something seems to need more mental effort and struggle. It probably does. If you're truly stuck, make a mental (or written) note of what piece you're missing, then go on to the next question. Your mind keeps working while your pen keeps moving, and often you'll have time later to go back and fill out these "reminders."

13. **Always stay till the bitter end.** If you finish early, go over previous answers. Correcting even one calculational error or adding even one idea or example can easily add a few points to your score. And you never know when you could use those extra points (like when you

get a 79 or an 89 and your school doesn't have pluses and minuses). Don't be psyched out by those people who leave after twenty minutes. Some of them have done so badly they're just throwing in the towel.

 BONUS TIP. When you get your test back, be sure to go over your instructor's comments one by one. This is one of the few times in the course you'll get customized feedback on your work. Don't waste this valuable resource by thinking it's too painful to look at the criticism. Who knows? There might even be words of encouragement. (Could happen. You never know.)

10 Tips for Writing the Perfect Paper

Like an architectural masterpiece or a well-crafted symphony, the perfect college paper is carefully constructed—rather than barfed out onto the page at 3 a.m. the night before. Each part is meticulously selected and polished up, then assembled with the others into a coherent and convincing whole. We should know. Between us, we've read tens of thousands of college papers—some perfect, others not so perfect—from which we've gleaned our ten best tips:

1. **Decide what kind of paper you're writing.** There's no one-size-fits-all in college. Some professors assign *research* papers, in which case you'll need to head to the library or to resources on the Internet (see "16 Techniques for Doing Research Like a Professor" on pp. 118–122). Other professors assign *analytical* papers (in which you're asked to analyze or evaluate some object, phenomenon, or text); in this case, you'll have to turn to your head for the answer. Still other professors assign a hybrid of the two, in which case you'll have to divide your labors. Know what type of assignment you're being asked to do before you start working on the paper.

2. **Answer exactly the question(s) asked.** Professors spend unbelievable amounts of time formulating the questions for the paper. Take the time to puzzle out precisely what's being asked. If there is more than one question or part asked, figure out how each question is different from the rest and what materials would be relevant to answering it.

 5-STAR TIP. Pay special attention to any verbs used in the paper assignment. *Compare, contrast, discuss, evaluate, explain, consider, formulate a hypothesis, raise an objection, argue for, trace, illustrate, defend,* and *summarize,* are all different tasks. Know which one(s) your professor is asking you to do—and what it would take to do it (or them). If you're not 100 percent, positively, absolutely, no doubt about it, sure, ask.

---

3. **Be sure to fill the space.** When a professor assigns a four- to six-page paper, he or she is usually expecting that the good papers will be more like six pages (while the students who don't know what to say will probably manage to fill only three or four pages). Worry more about writing too little than writing too much. (Of course, you should never exceed the page limit. That'll never make the professor happy.)

4. **Make sure your paper has a point.** Every paper should have a thesis—that is, a single point that is expressed in a single sentence. Without a thesis, a paper is just a report. And most college professors don't like reports. We think that this sentence should be the very first one in the paper, but some professors like you to write a brief introduction or "setup" paragraph (follow their instructions, if you get one of these profs). In any case, everyone would agree that the thesis sentence should come at least by the beginning of the second paragraph.

 BEST-KEPT SECRET. It's not enough to just state a thesis; you have to structure the whole paper around your thesis. Make sure each point you make in your paper supports the thesis you have advanced at the beginning of your paper. If you can't remember your thesis, refer back to it as you write.

5. **Give your paper direction.** A good paper moves through a series of steps that are arranged in some logical order. Make sure you have a reason for arranging your points in the order that you do—and that it is clear to the reader what that reason is. And make sure that each step does some work in advancing your argument. For each paragraph—then for each sentence within the paragraph—ask yourself: *Why is this here? How does it advance the overall argument?* And if your answer is "It doesn't," go back and take it out.

 EXTRA POINTER. Use "logical indicator" words such as *moreover, therefore, since, consequently, nevertheless, thus, then, now, first (second, third)*, to mark turning points in your argument. Not only will such "hinges" help your reader understand where your argument pivots, but they will also help you think out how it's structured.

6. **Write for a reasonably intelligent person—not the professor.** Many students make the mistake of writing for the professor— someone who already knows the answer and for whom a code word here or there will be more than enough. Write instead for a smart enough person who has not already taken the course. Take the time to explain each of your points fully—so that someone could understand what you mean just from what you write.

EXTRA POINTER. Be sure to explain any technical or unusual terms in ordinary language. Don't assume that the reader is a specialist in that field and will know what "etiological considerations" are.

7. **Avoid vagueness.** Many college papers suffer from being too general. They make many true claims, but express them in such an unspecific way that one can't really form a firm conception of what is being claimed. Be as particular as possible. And use specific and detailed examples—often more than one—to prove your points. Just like on the test.

8. **Have a quote quota.** In an analytical paper, it's usually not necessary to offer up elaborate quotes or sometimes even to quote at all. After all, it's *your* analysis that's being asked for. Even in a research paper, you should not use so many quotes that the paper becomes a mere summary or cataloguing of other people's work (see "16 Techniques for Doing Research Like a Professor" on pp. 118–122 for more on this topic).

IOHO. Generally, it's better to incorporate brief quotes, or portions of quotes, into your own sentences than to set off long citations in their own paragraphs. And be sure to always explain the quotes in your own words after you've reproduced them. The professor wants to know what you're seeing in the quote and what you take the quote to mean.

9. **Consolidate your argument.** As you read over the first drafts of your paper, consider taking out points that aren't central to the argument and developing more fully points that are. Often a more compact, more forcefully argued paper is a better paper; and, in any case, you should view your first draft as your first stab at properly capturing your idea, not the final, best-argued version.

10. **Deal the professor in.** There's nothing professors (or TAs) like more than helping good students construct excellent papers. Go to office hours with specific questions and problems, then follow up with e-mail as many times as is necessary or reasonable (for more on both these topics, see "The 15 Secrets of Going to See the Professor" on pp. 129–133 and "Etiquette for E-mailing Your Professor" on pp. 134–136).

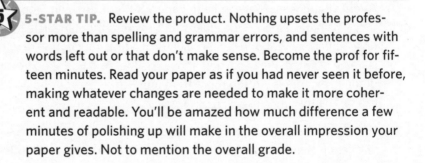

5-STAR TIP. Review the product. Nothing upsets the professor more than spelling and grammar errors, and sentences with words left out or that don't make sense. Become the prof for fifteen minutes. Read your paper as if you had never seen it before, making whatever changes are needed to make it more coherent and readable. You'll be amazed how much difference a few minutes of polishing up will make in the overall impression your paper gives. Not to mention the overall grade.

BONUS TIP. Know when to stop. At a certain point, endless revising serves no purpose (other than to make you upset). Indeed, it can weaken your paper by disrupting the natural flow of the points that you first wrote. If you tend to be a perfectionist, learn when to put your pen down. Or to click "Save" and "Send."

Top 10 Ways of Making the Leap from a B to an A

One of the most common questions we get asked is "What can I do to turn my B paper into an A?" This is one of the hardest things for a professor to put into words, since every case is different, and in any case there's often no one thing you need to do to get over the threshold from good to excellent work. Nevertheless, here are ten things you can do to increase your chances of bagging that much sought-after A:

#10. Offer a more subtle and nuanced thesis (rather than the most obvious one).

#9. Probe the relations between the parts of, or the issues treated in, the question.

#8. Give more examples or illustrations.

#7. Draw distinctions if they are relevant to the question(s) asked.

#6. Bring in material from the assigned readings or from extra articles selected in conjunction with the professor.

#5. Use the methods, techniques, and analytic tools of the field (like the ones the professor used in the class).

#4. Reach a firm conclusion (rather than wimping out).

#3. Pick a better topic next time—one that has more depth or about which you have more to say.

#2. Get feedback from the professor (or TA) as you're writing the paper (not after the fact, once you've gotten your B).

And the number-one tip for moving from a B to an A:

#1. Think harder. We know you can do better than this B paper.

16 Techniques for Doing Research Like a Professor

Once in a while you get hit with it. The dreaded fifteen- to twenty-five-page research paper, a.k.a. the term paper or semester project. This is your chance to join the community of the 20 percent or so of college professors who are actually doing research. How do they do it? And how can you? Have a look at our sixteen best tips for doing research—like a professor:

1. **Start from where you are.** The professor has his or her research program. You have the course. Carefully consider all the assigned paper topics, trying to pick one that seems interesting to you and about which you think you'll have something to say. If the professor is requiring you to propose a topic of your own, scour all the course materials—lecture notes, readings, syllabus, handouts, discussion sections, and course bibliography—for possible topics. Then meet with the prof to see if your proposed topic is one you could actually do, given what you know and what there is to know. A bad topic will not only net weeks of frustration, but a bad paper, in the end.

2. **Think e-.** Many up-to-date research materials are now available electronically. The best place to start is not Google, Bing, or Wikipedia, but with the *e-reserves* that the professor has listed. These are to be found at your school library's Web page under your particular course number (or sometimes at the course Web page). They have been carefully selected for relevance, level of depth, and general appropriateness for your particular course, so begin with them.

   Next stop is the *electronic resources* (or *e-resources*) at the library Web page. Usually they are divided into more general, though still scholarly, sources (such as InfoTrac, OneFile, LexisNexis Academic, and ProQuest); and more scholarly or "academic" sources (for example,

EbscoHost, Expanded Academic ASAP, JSTOR, Periodic Contents Index, Web of Science, and Web of Knowledge).

Another useful resource is the *subject guide*. Here, the databases are divided up by areas—all the way from aerospace engineering through women's studies. These can be incredibly helpful if you're just beginning to think about a topic.

To see an especially clear example of all these electronic resources, navigate to WWW.COLUMBIA.EDU/CU/LWEB/ERESOURCES.

EXTRA POINTER. When using e-resources, be sure to distinguish electronic *databases*, which are lists or directories of different journals, from *e-journals*, which are the actual journals or periodicals themselves (in electronic rather than print form).

BEST-KEPT SECRET. Always be on the lookout for top ten lists of databases at your library's Web page. These have been selected by librarians based on general usefulness or frequency of use by patrons and will in most cases work just great.

3. **Discover WorldCat.** One of the best resources is WWW.WORLDCAT.ORG, a free and public catalogue of more than a billion items available from more than ten thousand libraries worldwide. Best of all, you don't have to leave your house or dorm to use it: it's available in all modalities, including online and mobile (with downloadable apps for iPhone, Blackberry, and most Web-enabled phones). Check it out.

4. **Learn the shortcuts.** You'll have a much easier time conducting your search if you master advanced searching techniques. Use wildcard characters—typically a question mark (?), pound sign (#), or asterisk (*)—when you know only the first few letters of a word, or when you want to find all the words that start with a certain string of letters. Use the Boolean and-operator (typically AND or +) to limit the

results of a search, and the or-operator (OR or –) to expand the topic. And take out any apostrophes (O'Reilly) and replace foreign language characters that have diacritics (ç, ü) with their English equivalents (c, u, or ue).

5. **Use the living, breathing resources.** If twenty-first-century research is already giving you a headache, make your way to the reference desk at the brick-and-mortar library. The librarians there will be happy to help you with your electronic searches and might even walk you over to some of the (gasp) print books. At bigger universities, they even have reference librarians trained in specific study areas (humanities, social sciences, business, and natural sciences, for example). Use them.

6. **Learn about ILL.** If for whatever reason your library doesn't have some print book, or an e-jounral or article isn't available in any database, go to the interlibrary loan (ILL) department of your library. The folks there will happily get you the physical book or a copy of the article from another library, usually for free and in plenty of time for you to do your research paper (sometimes even on the same day, for electronic materials).

7. **Look for "gateway" sources.** It's often a good idea to start with broadly conceived sources that survey the problem, area, or subject you're researching and point the way to further, more specific studies. They might have names like *Cambridge Companion to X, Stanford Encyclopedia of Y, Grove Dictionary of Z,* or *Oxford Illustrated History of A.* (Ask your prof or TA for the best sources in your field). And whenever reading any source, look to the footnotes and bibliography for direction to further sources you might read.

8. **Drive your sources (don't let them drive you).** Always keep your investigation focused on the issue or problem you're studying. Just because some other guy makes some point—no matter how good it is—doesn't mean you have to include it in your paper, especially if the issue isn't really within the scope of your project. Keep in mind that you're the researcher here, so take control of the source material.

EXTRA POINTER. Keep it current. While every investigation is different, you should be attentive to the date of the source. Since, at least arguably, science and learning move forward, you might do better with an article dated August 2010 than one from the late 1890s. Besides, one of the things the professor might be looking for is your acquaintance with up-to-date journal research. (Of course, if you're studying primary sources—a fifteenth-century manuscript, nineteenth-century settlement records, or, if you're really lucky, a fourth-century B.C. Greek vase—older is better.)

9. **Embrace the Zen of research.** All research—and especially, good research—is a process that involves considerable uncertainty, doubt, and, often, the lack of quick or black-and-white answers. That's how discoveries are made. Get used to it. All of these are signs that the research is going well.

10. **Don't fixate too quickly.** Often in doing research—especially creative or original research—you'll find that your ideas change as you read new sources or think out an issue for yourself. This, too, is a good sign, and the process can be artificially aborted if you decide too soon on your final answer. Let ideas evolve naturally, and don't close the door too quickly on refining your ideas.

11. **Torture the data.** One of the main differences between superficial and really good research is that really good research picks something narrow to investigate, studies the topic in depth, and draws more nuanced or more meaningful conclusions about it. Of course, you should always consult with your professor or TA about how to conduct your research, but don't think of first-rate research simply as mindless collection and surveying of loads of data.

12. **Record and conquer.** Be sure to take complete and easily readable notes as you do your research. You'll never be able to keep straight what each of the authors has said if you don't have detailed records of what you've read. And be sure to keep complete bibliographical

citations (name of article, journal, author, page number, URL, and so on). You'll need that information later when you write your footnotes and compose your bibliography, and it's an incredible pain to have to find the sources again.

5-STAR TIP. Writing research papers will be 100 percent easier (or, at least, your paper will be 100 percent better organized) if you use reference-management software. If your college library doesn't provide it free, try Endnote, Refworks, Zotero, or Wizfolio (do a Web search to find the differences between each).

13. **Take a stand.** Your research should always culminate in some definite result or conclusion about what you've investigated. No real researcher—or, at least, no good real researcher—would conclude his or her study by saying "In the end, we can't be sure about...," or "Though I haven't shown this in this paper, my personal opinion is...." (These are real conclusions we've seen. Hey, you can't make up this stuff.)

14. **Fear not the footnote.** Some profs have a pole up their you-know-what about footnote styles. Why give them grief? Learn which of the many competing styles (APA, MLA, CBE, APSA, Turabian, and others) your professor thinks most important for the field. Techies and nerds will enjoy HTTP://MEMORIAL.LIBRARY.WISC.EDU/CITING.HTM. All the styles you'll ever want (and then some).

15. **Don't pad the bibliography.** Unless instructed otherwise, don't include in your bibliography sources you didn't use. Most likely your professor knows the literature and is interested only in how you used the materials.

16. **Leave time for writing.** It's one thing to do bang-up research, another to write a good research paper. Be sure to leave enough to time to write—and revise and edit—your paper. Rule of thumb: spend half the time researching, half the time writing.

6 PARTNERING WITH THE PROFESSOR

Y ou might think that taking a college course is just about going to class and hitting the books. And you wouldn't be wholly wrong. But you'll be most successful in your classes if you add some social networking into the mix. With your professor, that is. Developing a relationship with the prof can pay off in all sorts of ways. Maybe the professor can clear up a misconception that's causing you to leave each lecture in a fog of confusion. Maybe he or she can help you get the thesis of your paper right or tip you off to what's going to be on the exam—thus averting disaster. Or maybe it's some special consideration you need—an extension, a makeup exam, or the review of a grade—or perhaps just a little encouragement to get you through the course.

Whatever the case, you're going to have to approach your professor and interact with him or her. But students generally don't have much of an idea how to manage their relations with the professor. Some students are simply not interested in engaging the professor, while others see the teacher as an enemy to be avoided at all costs. And lots of students are terrified of going to an office hour, lest they somehow seem stupid or lost, or encounter a professor who has no interest in seeing them.

But it's well worth the time and effort to overcome these obstacles. It's really not that hard to interface well with your professor once you know how to do it—and once you understand the professor's perspective. And in the end, it'll make your educational experience exponentially better and—a few incompetent professors and SOBs notwithstanding—more fun, too.

In this chapter you'll learn:

▶ 15 Ways to Make Your Professor Love You

▶ The 15 Secrets of Going to See the Professor

▶ Etiquette for E-mailing Your Professor

▶ 10 Surefire Ways to Piss Off Your Professor

▶ Top 10 Things Professors Never Want to Hear (and What They Think When They Do Hear Them)

15 Ways to Make Your Professor Love You

Hey, professors are human beings, too. With real human feelings. How your professor feels about you can influence how much time he or she is willing to put in to help you with the course and even how good a recommendation he or she will write for grad school or a job. Surprisingly enough, only one in a hundred students thinks about this. Assuming you're one of the other ninety-nine, we offer you our fifteen best tips on how to ingratiate yourself to your professor:

1. **Look interested.** Professors like nothing better than to see alert and engaged students seated front and center in their classes. Even if they're usually too polite to mention it, professors do notice students who sit there yawning or looking bummed out—or, worse yet, openly texting or reading e-mail. If you look as if you're following, actively taking notes, and showing an interest in the material, you'll stand out from the huddled masses.

2. **Say hi to the professor when he or she enters the room.** Seems obvious, but take a look around sometime to see how few students do it.

3. **Ask a question.** Most professors regularly interrupt their presentations to give students a chance to ask questions. And when professors do, they're hoping for some kind of response—not the apathetic silence that often greets them. Your question will light up your professor's day. Make sure it's a question about the material, not one of these much-hated questions like: "Will this be on the test?" "Could you repeat what you just said for the past fifteen minutes?" or "When is the paper due?"

EXTRA POINTER. Bonus points will be given if your question demonstrates an understanding of material presented in an earlier class. Your professor will think, "Wow—a student who came to class and actually remembers something from last week!" Also good is when your question shows an acquaintance with the reading. Your professor will think, "Wow—someone is actually poring over that dull-as-dishwater textbook I assigned!"

4. **Put in your two cents' worth.** Another way professors break the monotony of the fifty-minute lecture is by themselves asking questions of the students. At times, running a class discussion can be like pulling teeth. So you're sure to win the professor's favor if you pipe up with an answer (or at least a stab at an answer) to the professor's query. And don't be afraid to be the first one in, either. Professors understand that it's sometimes hard to think on your feet.

5-STAR TIP. Do not take this as a green light to offer up whatever thought you have, no matter how dumb or unrelated to the question asked. If you just shoot your mouth off, without giving any thought at all to what you're saying, you're likely to become a major thorn in your professor's side and incur the wrath of your fellow students.

5. **Volunteer first.** You have a golden opportunity to earn your prof's affections if you are the first to volunteer when your professor is dividing up tasks for later in the semester—for example, seminar presentations, debates, or discussion leaders. Some professors even give special breaks on the grading for those brave enough to step up to bat first.

6. **Continue the conversation outside of class.** You will surely get on your professor's good side if you approach him or her outside of class to talk about issues raised in class. Usually the best venue is during office hours, but some professors have time to chat before or after class. Keep in mind that the more you can display your interest in the course material for its own sake (rather than for a good grade on the

paper or test), the better. If you are shy, an e-mail to the professor
following up on some issue raised in class can also do the trick (for
tips on this approach, see "Etiquette for E-mailing Your Professor" on
pp. 134–136).

7. **Read the comments.** You can't imagine how many students come to
office hours to go over a paper or test and haven't even read the professor's comments. Professors especially appreciate those students
who have, because it shows that you actually want to learn from
what the professor has to say. And it's a time-saver for the prof, too:
Who wants to say again what they just finished writing down the
night before? (Also see "The 15 Secrets of Going to See the Professor," coming up on pp. 129–133.)

8. **Join the team.** Some professors offer students the opportunity to
work with them on a joint research project or do an internship. This
can be one of the best ways to forge a great relationship with your
professor and gain valuable training in your field. If no research or
internship opportunities are available, at least see if you can take
a small class or seminar with some professor you would like to
work with.

9. **Ask the prof what he or she is working on.** Many professors spend
lots of years working on a research project. And there's almost nothing professors like to talk about more than their research. But it's a
rare student who thinks to ask the professor about it. This is something that'll surely set you off from the crowd, and, hey, you might
even learn something about Siberian poetry of the late 1820s or the
synthesis of amino acids.

10. **Participate in departmental activities.** Professors will take note of
you when they see you at departmental events such as outside lectures, colloquia, or meetings of the departmental student club. Your
participation shows you really care about the field. (Professors are
suckers for that sort of thing.)

11. **Alert your professor to current events related to the class.** Bringing in a newspaper item or Web article that has relevance to the
course is a surefire way to win approval from your professor. Not
only does he or she see that you are engaged enough with the class

to recognize its relevance to real-world activities, but it gives the professor some valuable ammunition to prove to the rest of the class that—despite what they've been thinking—someone actually finds the course useful or interesting.

12. **Congratulate the professor on an achievement.** If you read on the college Web site or student newspaper that your professor just published a book, won an award, or has gotten tenure and/or promotion, it's a very nice thing to offer congratulations. Everyone likes his or her accomplishments recognized, even professors.

13. **Tell your prof you like the class.** Students rarely realize that professors worry about how a class is going, and would desperately like to hear that students are enjoying it. Look for an occasion when you can slip in, in a casual but sincere way, that you like the class. It would be a special touch if you could come up with some specific thing about the class that you are enjoying, but even a general expression of appreciation would surely be welcome.

 EXTRA POINTER. It's one thing to compliment a professor and another to lay it on too thick. Once you slip into sucking up mode, the professor realizes it's more about you trying to get a good grade than about him or her being a good professor. Never a good idea.

14. **Thank the professor when he or she does you a favor.** You might not realize it, but professors aren't obligated to do a lot of the things they do for students. Like making special appointments, answering e-mails on evenings and weekends, giving extensions and makeups, and providing help with picking other courses in the department. Professors remember the students who thank them—in person or at least by e-mail—for any special considerations that the professor might have offered. Which will come in very handy when you need another favor or two.

15. **Always be positive.** Whenever you have any interaction with the professor—whether in the class, in the office, or even in the hall— always be upbeat and enthusiastic. No one likes a sourpuss.

The 15 Secrets of Going to See the Professor

One of the best things you can do any time in the semester is go see the professor. So hoof on over to an office hour and have some one-on-one face time with someone who'll help you master the material and improve your grade, to boot. But how should you conduct this tête-à-tête with the prof? Here are fifteen insider tips about how to make that office hour really count:

1. **Have no fear.** No need to get all bent out of shape about going to see the professor. The prof would actually *like* to see you and answer your questions. Believe it or not, he or she is on your side and is eager to see you do well. And besides, he or she has seen many students stupider than you, so nothing you're going to ask will set the record for stupidity.

EXTRA POINTER. Don't assume the professor will think, "I've taught this before, so why didn't this dumb-ass student get it?" Professors know that the material is difficult and sometimes goes by pretty quickly in lecture, so they'll be happy to explain it again. Just don't ask them to go over *all* of it.

---

2. **Go it alone.** Even though you might feel more comfortable going with a friend or partner, the office hour will go better if it's just you and the professor. You'll get in more questions, the discussion will be tailored to what you need most help on, and two-party communication is almost always more productive than committee work. Your friend can wait outside for the postmortem.

3. **Go while there's still time.** It's best to go as early as a week or two before the test is to be held or the paper is due. That way you'll have plenty of time to apply the suggestions the professor might make. And you'll avoid the interminable line of students outside the office the day before the assignment comes due.

4. **Don't make 'em wait.** If you can't make the official office hours, most professors are willing to make individual appointments to help you out. If you're lucky enough to land such an accommodation, though, be sure you're 100 percent on time. There's nothing that ticks off a professor more than making him- or herself available for a custom office hour only to find that you don't care enough to come on time. And besides, the professor might leave after ten minutes, which would make your trip a total loss. (See our "10 Surefire Ways to Piss Off Your Professor" on pp. 137–140 for nine more ways to get on your prof's bad side.)

5. **Come ready to work.** If you're meeting with the professor to go over a paper or test, or to ask questions about a particular lecture or reading, make sure you bring that paper or test, or your lecture notes or a copy of the article. The prof doesn't remember the comments he or she wrote on your individual piece of work—though he or she will be able to recall them after just a brief glance at your work. And if you have your lecture notes or the article in hand, you and the prof will be able to examine specific points that are confusing to you, rather than just talking in a general way about the contents.

6. **Come in with something to say.** Office hours almost always go better if you bring a few specific questions to the meeting. It's almost never good to start a meeting with general comments such as: "I didn't understand what you said about [main topic of the course]" or "I couldn't understand any of your lectures last week." Much better is to come in with two or three conversation-starters about a specific concept, point, or problem you didn't understand. Keep in mind that in a fifteen-minute office hour (which is how long these things usually last), two or three questions are usually the most you'll have time to discuss.

5-STAR TIP. Go for the meat. It's usually best to ask questions about the main ideas, rather than about little facts or tiny details. Focusing on the central and most far-reaching issues will also help you on the test or paper, because professors usually ask about the most important points, not picayune details.

7. **Start the conversation yourself...** You've come to have your concerns addressed. You should start the conversation by asking a question or raising an issue.

   ...But let the man (or woman) talk. Be sure you also let the professor get a word in edgewise. Sometimes students come in prepared with so many things to say that the professor never gets a chance to get his or her two cents in. Net result? You don't get the benefit of the professor's suggestions and guidance, which is—when you think about it—what you came for. Key clue: when the professor starts talking, no matter how briefly and how tentatively, you stop talking. Always works.

8. **Follow up with follow-ups.** Once you've gotten a good discussion going, it's good to probe issues more fully by asking directed questions about what the professor just said. The most productive office hours occur when new—and unexpected—ideas are generated during the conversation. Your follow-ups, even when you're not sure where the discussion is going, will help generate such ideas.

9. **Don't be coy.** No point being shy or pretending. If the professor says something you don't understand (or directs your attention to something in the lecture or reading that you can't identify), it's always good to say, simply and forthrightly, that you haven't understood. Professors, who have often gone over the same material with different students, simply don't realize that you're not taking in what they just said. And they'll appreciate your honesty and real desire to learn.

10. **Don't dispute balls and strikes.** It's perfectly all right to go to the professor and ask why you got the grade you did. It's not all right to mount a pitched battle with the professor about each point the

grader took off. A better idea would be to focus on the concepts you didn't understand—and on the (less-than-successful) strategies you used in writing the paper or taking the test—so that you can do better next time.

BEST-KEPT SECRET. Most professors, when they smell a grade dispute coming, do the best they can to shut down the discussion. Keep this in mind when you shift the discussion from the course material to why you got the grade you did (often not worth it).

11. **Get it down.** It's always a good idea to take notes. Points often go by very fast in conversation, and you'll be pleased to have a record of what the professor suggested when it comes time for writing the paper or studying for the test. And don't be embarrassed, either: professors themselves are very used to taking notes at meetings.

EXTRA POINTER. If the professor suggests additional readings or reference materials, make sure you get down as full and exact a citation as you can. You'd be amazed how often students can't find the article afterwards because they've written down only a few key words (or misspelled the author's name).

12. **Don't make it personal.** It's almost never a good use of office time to confess your personal troubles, problems with your life, your roommate, your family, and so on. The professor is not a confidant, and even if he or she were, airing your problems in this venue won't help you in the course.

13. **Ask and ye shall receive (maybe).** It's generally not such a great idea to ask for an extension or a makeup exam (either of which just puts off the pain). But sometimes such accommodations would really, really, really help you out (for example, when you've got two other exams on that day). Always ask. Politely, of course. Sometimes professors have hidden course policies that allow them latitude for such special cases. And what's the worst that can happen? They'll turn you down.

14. **Be a mensch.** It's always nice—and prudent, too—to politely greet the professor with an upbeat "Hello, Professor So and So" at the beginning of the meeting and to thank him or her at the close for taking the time to meet with you. Professors respond to such niceties, especially when you mean them.

15. **Beg for more.** It's often good to try to set up an additional meeting if you still have questions and would like to continue the discussion. And don't forget about e-mail. Professors are often very happy to answer (specific and focused) questions by e-mail or even to read drafts or at least paragraphs of papers before you hand them in.

 BEST-KEPT SECRET. Many professors are starting to use Skype as a way of communicating with students outside of office hours. Ask if your professor is one of them.

Bottom line? Office hours are one of the most high-value but underutilized resources at college. Take advantage of this unique opportunity.

Etiquette for E-mailing Your Professor

Professors, like everyone else, have gone electronic, which means that in addition to the one-on-one office hour, they're increasingly willing to communicate by e-mail. Here are some things to consider before clicking "Send":

▶ **E-mail is forever.** Once you send it off, you can't get it back. Once your professor has it, he or she owns it and can save it, or, in the worst case, forward it on to colleagues for a good laugh. At your expense.

▶ **E-mail goes where it's told.** Check—and double check—to see that the right address appears in the "To" line. Just because your mom and your professor are both named Lynn is no reason to send all your love to Professor Lynn.

▶ **Professors might not be using the cruddy university e-mail system.** So send it to the address they actually use, not the one on the university directory. (Check the syllabus or assignment sheet for clues.)

▶ **Professors might not open mail sent from luckydogpig@ thepound.com.** They prefer to open mail sent from more reputable addresses, like your.name@theCruddyUniversityE-mail System.edu.

▶ **Subject lines are for subjects.** Put a brief explanation of the nature of the e-mail (like "question about paper") in the subject line. Never include demands such as "Urgent request: immediate response needed." That's the surest way to get your request trashed.

▶ **Salutations matter.** The safest way to start is with "Dear Professor So and So" (using their last name). That way you won't be getting into the issue of whether the prof has a PhD or not, and you won't seem sexist when you address your female professor as Ms. or, worse yet, Mrs. This and That.

► **Clear and concise is best.** Your prof might get twenty-five to thirty e-mails a day. So it's best if you ask your questions in as focused and succinct a way as possible (hint: it's often good to number your questions). And if your question is very elaborate or multifaceted, it's best to go to an in-person office hour. You'll get better service that way.

EXTRA POINTER. Before sending a draft of a paper to a professor as an attachment, confirm that he or she is willing to accept such long documents. If not, find out whether he or she will look over a page or even a central paragraph of your work incorporated into the body of the e-mail. And be sure to cc yourself any time you send a piece of work—who knows the fate of the document you're sending?

5-STAR TIP. Never e-mail your paper as an attachment in a bizarre format. You might think that .odt is a really cool file extension, since you didn't have to pay for Open Office. But if it takes the professor twenty minutes to find the plug-in (which doesn't work), then another half-hour to download Open Office (which ties up way too much space on his or her computer), what was supposed to be a fifteen-minute grading job on your paper is now taking over an hour. And then the prof has to assign your grade. Recommendation: stick to Word.

► **Always acknowledge.** If your professor deigns to answer—or send you the handout or reference that you asked for—be sure to tell him or her that you got it. That way he or she will think kindly of you next time you need something.

► **THIS IS NOT A SHOUTING MATCH.** Don't write in all uppercase letters (which is an e-mail convention for anger or other strong emotion). No one likes being yelled at.

► **No one really likes emoticons and smileys.** Trust us on this one. ☺

▶ **This is not Facebook.** So don't write the professor in the same way you'd write on your friend's wall.

5-STAR TIP. It's never a good idea to "poke" your professor. No matter how funny it seems at the time.

▶ **This is not IMing.** So pls dun wrte yor profeSR llk ur txtN. uz abbrz @ yor own rsk. coRec me f lm wrng. (Translation thanks to WWW.TRANSL8IT.COM, which features a neat little Facebook widget.)

▶ **This is not CollegeHumor.com.** So resist the temptation to talk about the "badass" paper you need help with, your "loser" TA who didn't teach you what you needed to know, or the "crappy" grade you just got on the midterm.

▶ **This is not RateMyProfessors.com.** The professor doesn't want your comments about his or her performance in the class. Save those for the end-of-semester evaluations, where you'll be able to spout off. Anonymously.

▶ **Spelling mistakes make you look like a doofus.** So always use the spel check and proofread yyour e-mail, two.

▶ **Sign-offs and signatures count.** Always end by thanking the professor for his or her time and closing with "Best wishes" or "Regards" (or some other relatively formal, but friendly closing). And always sign with your (entire) real name, not some wacky nickname like Ry-Ry or Biff.

▶ **Your prof doesn't want to hear your philosophy of life.** Skip the cute quotes or statements of your religious or political views at the bottom of your e-mail. You never know what offends.

▶ **Don't lay it on too thick.** It's one thing to be polite and friendly in your e-mail; it's another thing to wind up with a brown nose.

10 Surefire Ways to Piss Off Your Professor

Like any other relation between two people, the student-professor interaction depends on goodwill from both sides. Things go wrong when one party—for example, the student—does something that offends the other party—for example, the professor. In some cases, the student isn't even aware that he or she has done something to irritate the prof. Lest you unwittingly make a misstep, here are ten of the most common ways students get on the wrong side of their professors—and how you can avoid these *faux pas*:

1. **Making excuses for missing class.** Many students feel guilty when, for whatever reason, they don't show up for class. But the last thing in the world the professor wants to know is that your family reunion was more important than his or her class, or that your cramming for your P-Chem exam took precedence over yet another boring lecture. Suggestion: carefully think out what excuses you're going to make for missing class or, better yet, don't make any excuses at all.

 EXTRA POINTER. If you must make an excuse, either because the professor takes attendance or because he or she asks you why you weren't there, it's best to be as brief as possible. Simply saying that you weren't feeling well, that your kid was sick, or that there was an accident on the freeway will work well.

2. **Misbehaving in class.** It's very easy for students to think that the prof pays no attention to what they are doing in a lecture. The class is huge, so why should the teacher even care what the audience is doing? Surprisingly enough, though, the professor often notices—and sometimes remembers—the student who's busy IMing in class or whose cell phone goes off or, worst of all, who nods off during

class. And while few professors will dock your grade for such questionable behavior, it can come back to bite you when you need some help with a paper, an extension of a deadline, or when your score is on the borderline between two grades.

3. **Challenging your professor publicly.** It's one thing to ask a pointed question or propose a different interpretation; it's another thing to suggest (however implicitly) that the professor has no idea what he or she is talking about or that no one has understood anything he or she has said so far. Before asking a question in lecture, make sure you're not going to show the professor up or otherwise embarrass him or her. It's not worth it.

4. **Disputing a grade like a "mad dog."** Even though it's the least pleasant part of the job, all professors realize they're obligated to entertain student questions and disputes about their grades. But professors really hate it when some student comes in frothing at the mouth and complaining that the grade on their paper is unacceptable, unfair, wrong—or all of the above. One likely result of such behavior: the professor will reread your paper like a gymnastics judge at the Olympics, replaying everything in slo mo, looking for any possible deduction. And in many cases will come to the conclusion that the initial grade was way too high for such a lousy piece of work. Tip: consider the dispute from the side of the interaction that counts. The professor's.

5. **Seeming really stupid.** From time to time professors encounter stupidity the likes of which they've never seen. Students who can't remember who painted the Mona Lisa. Students who say they can't come to a 12:30 p.m. office hour because it's in the middle of the night. And students who don't know their "its" from their "it's," even though the third graders in town have it on their spelling lists this week. Seeing this kind of stupidity from college students can really tick off a professor. (On the positive side, it does make for some great cocktail party snickering with the professor's faculty friends.)

6. **Giving lame excuses for handing in a late paper or missing an exam.** Some excuses wear really thin with professors. Computer ate your paper (have you ever heard of backups?). Alarm clock didn't go off (as if I've never heard that one before). Grandmother died

(amazing how many grandmothers go to meet their maker the day of the midterm). But some excuses really go off the deep end. Like a student who vehemently argued that he was never told about a course rule because his syllabus was missing a page—all the while holding that very page in his hands. On the flip side, the best excuses we've heard include: "I couldn't get to the test because I was in jail" (how can you argue with that one?) and "I couldn't do the paper because Ozarks Electric hasn't restored the power to my house fifteen days after the ice storm" (it's true).

7. **Treating the professor like your servant.** You're guaranteed to offend the professor if you leave phone messages or send e-mail that say: ABSOLUTELY MUST SEE YOU TOMORROW TO DISCUSS MY EXAM. I HAVE CLASSES FROM 10:30 TO 12:30, LUNCH WITH MY FRAT 'TIL 2 AND HAVE TO WORK FROM 3 TO 5. SO I AM AVAILABLE BETWEEN 2 AND 3. PLEASE RESPOND IMMEDIATELY. Yeah, right.

8. **Plagiarizing in super-obvious ways.** No professor likes students who cheat. But worse even than plagiarism is copying in a way that's so transparent and obvious that anyone with half a brain could detect it. Like what happens when the professor enters the first few words of your paper into a Google search and finds, word for word, parts of your paper in the first entry. Look—professors think plagiarism is intellectual stealing and, as the antilittering signs in New York City say, "disgusting and filthy, so don't do it." But you add insult to injury when you copy in so obvious a way that your professor would have to be a moron not to be able to find your source.

9. **Comparing your prof to other profs.** No professor wants to hear how he or she stacks up against other professors you've had or against professors teaching other sections of the course. Even a casual comparison can offend, so think before you compare.

10. **Going over your prof's head.** No prof will be happy if you go to the department chair (or worse yet, the dean) with complaints about the course or about how the professor is treating you. But it's possible to wind up offending through no intention of your own. Say, you encounter the department chair, either in the hall or at

a departmental function, and he or she asks you, "So, how's that course X with Professor Y going?" You answer, "Not so great, given A, B, C, and D." After which, the next time the chair sees that prof, he or she says, "So I hear your course X is having some problems," and when asked, casually mentions your name as the source of the "observations." You wind up in the doghouse with the prof, when all you intended was to be friendly with the departmental chair. Moral? Be careful where you bad-mouth your professor—what you say can come back to bite you.

Top 10 Things Professors Never Want to Hear (and What They Think When They Do Hear Them)

#10. **"I missed class yesterday. So did you do anything important?"**

Of course not. I just stood up in front and ran my mouth about nothing, like I always do.

#9. **"I lost the syllabus. Oh, and the paper assignment, too. Would you mind e-mailing them to me?"**

Sure, last time I checked my job description, it included research, teaching, and being at your beck and call.

#8. **"Can we go over my test?"**

Don't you think reading the whole thing through once was more than enough for me?

#7. **"I'm terribly sorry my paper wasn't in on time; my dog ate my printer."**

Time for obedience training. For you.

#6. **"My friend and I worked together on this paper. How come I got a B and he got an A?"**

Hmm, in addition to being better looking than you, your friend is also smarter.

#5. **"I really need an A in this class."**

Well, if I were parceling out A's on the basis on need, I'd be giving them to all those D students. They need 'em more than you.

#4. **"This C is totally unacceptable to me. I'm an A student."**

Not in my class.

#3. **"I'm leaving early for my ski vacation. So can I take the final early?"**

Now there's a deal I can't refuse: I do double-work making two finals, and you spend more quality time on the slopes.

#2. **"I'd do anything for an A."**

Anything?

And the number-one thing professors never want to hear:

#1. **"B-minus? You've got to be kidding. I paid good money for that paper."**

7 EMERGENCY 9-1-1

College is not always a luxury cruise. Sometimes it's more like a boat that's sprung a few leaks. Or worse, one that's taking on water and about to take a Titanic-like plunge to the bottom. When you see signs of major trouble, it's easy to start the blame game: it's the college's fault, or the professors', or (if you're in a really confessional mood) my own. Then, panic sets in: *OMG, what should I do next? Everyone is doing better than me. How will I survive this semester?* And finally, sometimes, one wants to simply give up on the whole thing: *I'm never going to be able to do college. I shouldn't even be here. Where's the exit?*

We advise a different course. Instead of going off the deep end, make a careful, rational assessment of what's gone wrong, then make a plan to fix things up. This chapter can help. The tips here cover a wide range of problems—some that might come up early in the semester, others that tend to hit around the midterm, still others that arise only when the semester is in its dying throes. Even when the situation looks hopeless, a few practical, and sometimes surprisingly simple, techniques can turn the thing around.

In this chapter you'll learn:

- ▶ 10 Things to Do When You Can't Keep Up with the Lecture
- ▶ Top 10 Signs You've Been Cutting Too Many Classes
- ▶ Bombed the Midterm: Now What?
- ▶ 7 Best Last-Minute Strategies for Saving Your Grade
- ▶ 10 Signs You're in Real Trouble at College
- ▶ What, Then, to Do? The 7-Step Approach

10 Things to Do When You Can't Keep Up with the Lecture

One of the biggest—and most common—problems students have at college is not being able to keep up with the lecturer. No matter how much you try, you're always a few steps behind and never quite able to get it all down. What to do? Consider our ten tips for getting your note taking up to speed:

1. **Hear clearly.** It's very difficult to take good notes when you can't clearly hear all that the professor is saying (even the words he or she is muttering under his or her breath). So pick a seat that's in direct earshot of the lecturer. And keep in mind that since bodies absorb sound, it'll be harder to hear when the room is full and when your compatriots are also muttering under their breath.

2. **Come prepared.** Doing the reading or polishing off the problem set before the lecture will give you important advance information on what the lecture is going to be about. It's easier to follow and take notes on a lecture when you know what it's going to cover.

 EXTRA POINTER. If weird names and foreign terms are giving you trouble, prepare a cheat sheet with important names and terms and bring it with you to the class. This will save you having to figure out on the spot how to spell these things—thereby saving you valuable note-taking time. Some students even devise three-letter abbreviations for exotic names of people and places.

 5-STAR TIP. Be sure to check the syllabus (including any schedule of readings and lectures) and the course Web page for lists of topics, and sometimes even outlines, of what's going to be taken up in lecture. The more information you have in advance—especially about the central points and the structure of the lecture—the easier it'll be to get it all down.

3. **Don't take mental breaks.** As long as the professor is up there dishing out material, keep focused on what's being said and get it down into your notes. Now's not the time to be zoning in and out (save that for your study time when you're in control of the speed at which the content is being presented).

4. **Write fast—really fast.** Most college students can text with blazing speed with just two thumbs, but when it comes to note taking the old-fashioned way, they shift into a paralyzingly slow pace. Write in script as messy as you can read and use whatever shorthand will make sense to you. (Keep in mind that it'll have to make sense to you at 11 p.m. the night before the test, so don't go overboard.) Or use a laptop, tablet, or netbook. Especially good for note taking are netbooks, which typically weigh less than three pounds, have an eight-hour battery, are about two-thirds the size of a normal laptop, and will set you back only $300. (For our most current recommendations, check out WWW.PROFESSORSGUIDE.COM/TECHRECS.)

5. **Capture the professor's thoughts, not his or her exact words.** Note taking is not about creating a word-for-word transcript of the lecture, but getting down the main ideas (and the most important details) of what the professor has said. So don't waste time trying to decide if the prof noted "close parallels" or "lots of similarities" between this and that. Trust us, the professor isn't going to remember the exact language, so you don't need to either.

 EXTRA POINTER. Of course, if it's a key technical term, a crucial distinction, or a theorem or equation in a problem, it is important to get down word-for-word what the professor is saying. Try to focus 100 percent on what the professor is saying at these points, and be sure to copy down (as fast as you can) anything he or she writes on the board or uncovers in a PowerPoint.

6. **Look for importance—and structure.** In any given lecture, not every point is of equal significance: some are the key ideas, some are expansion and embellishment, some are examples or illustrations,

and some are just things that occur to the professor as he or she is talking. Moreover, in any lecture the points are put together in a certain order and with a certain direction and logic: there usually is a reason that points come at the place they do and stand in the relations they do. Always be on the lookout for the most important points and their structure. If you can locate the key points of the lecture and figure out their arrangement, it'll be ten times easier to take notes.

7. **Don't panic too soon.** Professors almost always sum up and repeat the main points at various times in the lectures, so if you missed something the first time around, it's likely to come back again. The summary at the end of that section or at the end of the lecture can be particularly useful if you missed a point the first time around.

8. **Keep practicing.** With note taking, as with most things in life, practice makes perfect. As you keep at it, and as you get more accustomed to your professor's lecturing style, your notes will get better.

REALITY CHECK. A good time to check whether you're getting down enough material—and the right points—of the lecture is after the first test. If you see many things on the exam that were talked about in lecture but did not make it into your notes, you should try to diagnose the problems you're having in taking good notes. And for many students it's a good idea to go see the professor or TA—armed with your notes, of course—to see what suggestions they might have about improving your note-taking techniques. Teachers are often surprisingly interested in seeing how well their students are getting down the main points and often will be very willing to offer suggestions about how to take better notes.

9. **Use "aids."** If you're really having trouble taking notes, it might be useful seeing whether official lecture notes are sold at the bookstore (many universities have these for beginning classes). And you might ask the professor if you could record the class so you can listen to it, with breaks, at your leisure. Just don't get too addicted to these aids.

Since the real skill is learning to take notes yourself, these short-term fixes aren't to your advantage in the long term.

 IOHO. Recently a number of online note-taking services and communities have arisen. We think that, while in theory these could be good, in practice they're not so great to get started with. It's easier to cut class if you think someone else in the community will be doing your dirty work for you. And besides, the note-takers could be significantly less good students than you. Most important, note taking yourself is one of the key ways you're actively processing, and learning, the material. So suck it up and do it yourself. Leave the social networking for *social* networking.

---

10. **In the worst case, bail.** If, after trying all these tips, you still can't keep up with the note-taking, maybe the problem isn't your note-taking skills, but that the class is too hard for you. If so, forget about improving your note taking, and drop the class. No shame in that.

Top 10 Signs You've Been Cutting Too Many Classes

#10. You show up Wednesday at 9 a.m. only to find the class meets Tuesdays and Thursdays from 3 to 4 p.m.

#9. You're so confused by the lecture that you can't get in your usual Z's.

#8. Your classmates roll their eyes when you do show up and "contribute" to the discussion.

#7. You ask when the midterm is going to be, only to find out it was held three weeks ago.

#6. It's the tenth week of the semester and the prof mistakes you for a prospective student.

#5. You ask the professor what you can do to catch up, and he or she starts laughing like a hyena.

#4. You discover that while you were gone your Russian class has mysteriously moved from singing the alphabet to reading *War and Peace*—in its entirety.

#3. The hottie you had you eye on is now married to the guy at the end of the row.

#2. You find a really interesting class for next semester, then realize you're currently in it.

And the number-one sign you've been cutting too many classes:

#1. You arrive at the final only to find out that the professor gave an in-class final and the course is already over.

 the Midterm: Now What?

It's the eighth week of the semester and you thought you were doing great. But you just got back your midterm and, can you believe it, it's a C (or worse). Panic sets in. *Drop out of college? Crawl back home to your parents?* Here are some better ideas:

▶ **Figure out the real score.** Sure, you know you got a 75 on the midterm. But have you considered the impact of that mess-up on your total grade in the course? Though you may not have thought about it in your shroud of despair, in many courses the midterm counts one quarter or less of the whole course grade. That's because most professors want to give students a chance to screw up and still have some motivation to keep working throughout the course. So all may not be lost—yet.

▶ **Ignore the neighbors.** Despite what you have been able to glean by glancing surreptitiously at other folks' A-papers, you are not the only one in the class with a lousy grade. So don't assume that everybody is doing better than you. They're not.

▶ **Don't miss the going-over-the-test.** No matter how bad you think the test went, don't duck out on the day the tests are returned (or the section meeting that week). That's the time when most professors (or TAs) can't help but whine, berate, or tell the class how badly they did—all the while revealing the components of the perfect answer. This is a golden opportunity for you to see what they were really looking for. So listen up—and take notes.

 EXTRA POINTER. Pay special attention when the professor lists points that could have gone into the good answer. Get most of these points, you'd have had an A, half or more, a B, and not too many at all, some sort of C. Live and learn.

▶ **Look in the rearview mirror.** Now is the time to figure out what went wrong in your preparation, so that you can correct it before the next test (which probably will be quite similar to this one). Pinpoint your problems. Did you miss key lectures or not fully understand the lectures? Did you skip the reading or focus too heavily on it? Did you blow off studying, study in the wrong way, or study with the wrong comrades? Did you fail to answer exactly what was being asked or make mistakes in your answers? Figure it all out, and you'll do better next time.

▶ **Feed on the feedback.** Your test will no doubt come back with plenty of red ink marking places where you lost points and, if you're lucky, loads of comments saying how you could have done better. This is your individualized interface with the prof, so read your teacher's words of wisdom with great care. Yeah, these comments were written pretty quickly while your prof was struggling to get through the stack and get on with his or her life. But the professor was still focusing on your work—one of the few times this happens in the typical semester.

 EXTRA POINTER. Give the grader the benefit of the doubt. Things will go better if you read the comments with the aim of learning how to improve, instead of demonstrating how incompetent the grader is.

▶ **Get some face time.** A trip to your professor's office hours—or, in some cases your TA's—can provide a fount of knowledge about how to avert future disasters. Professors regularly see students seeking help after getting bad grades, so why let your friends with the C's get a leg up on you?

BEST-KEPT SECRET. Professors will usually really open up and offer all sorts of aid if you go to them and say, "I didn't do so well on the midterm and I see from the comments that... Could you explain a little more fully how I might correct this problem on the next test?" (Shows that you've read the comments, are not angry, and would like to improve). Less good: "I'd like to go over my test and see why I got the grade I did." (Professors think that's what the comments were supposed to accomplish). Least good: "Here's my exam—could you find some extra points for me?" (Professors think grade grubbing is your job.)

▶ **Turn over a new leaf.** Now's the time to make strategic changes. The ones that will address the specific ways things went wrong. Not changes your parents, friends, and even advisers suggest, without having a clue about what you did right and what you did wrong. Above all, don't keep using the old strategies that got you into deep doo-doo in the first place.

▶ **Lighten the load.** In some cases, dropping the course might be the right thing to do—like when you're so far behind that you can never catch up, even if you studied day and night for the rest of the semester—or where the skill level kicks up a notch or two after the midterm (for example, in a language course or math class). And don't worry—there's nothing wrong with a W (for withdrawal) on your record. There's much more wrong with a grade that sucks.

Best Last-Minute Strategies for Saving Your Grade

Sometimes even the best-laid plans go wrong. And sometimes you never had a plan in the first place. But whatever the reason, toward the end of the semester some college students find themselves in a ginormous hole. But there's no reason to fold just yet, at least not before checking out our seven things to do to salvage your semester:

1. **The extension.** Even if the due date for the paper is accompanied by copious threats, many professors will give students extra time to complete a paper. To get an extension, you have to ask. Make your request face-to-face (no e-mail, Twitter, Facebook, or snail-notes) and during an official office hour, not before or after class. Explain your reasons simply and concisely: a sob story is OK if it's believable and no more than twenty seconds long. Be honest and supernice: these qualities can outweigh even a flimsy excuse. And propose a firm date for completion of the work—say an extra week or two. Tests are more dicey: many professors aren't even allowed to give makeup exams. But ask anyway. You never know...

BEST-KEPT SECRET. At many schools you're entitled to an automatic extension if you have more than two finals on the same day. Be sure to ask if you find yourself in this situation.

2. **The incomplete.** If you're way, way, behind—or missing more than one piece of work—an extension won't do the trick. What you need is an incomplete—that is, an I in the course plus several months to complete the work (often the university sets the completion date as some particular week of the next semester). Incompletes may temporarily appear on your record, but they'll go away when you submit

the outstanding work. The real drawback, though, is that they are a bear to complete outside the structure of the class. Many a student happily goes off with an incomplete, only to see it lapse to an F when he or she never gets the energy or motivation to finish the work in the allotted time.

3. **The withdrawal.** In cases where you have a sudden or serious situation—an accident, serious illness, or family emergency—you may be eligible to withdraw from a class. This is often the best solution when you have not been able to do any or most of the work in a class. Keep in mind that withdrawals are often controlled by the dean or registrar's office (rather than the professor) and are subject to strict rules. In some schools, past a certain date you may be required to withdraw from the entire semester (which is good if you have done no work in any course, but not so good if you are behind in only one course). And keep in mind that in most cases there are no refunds. Makes it hard to just walk away from the semester.

4. **The suck-it-up.** You might find that the best solution is to just take an F on one piece of work in the class and see if you can still eke by with the remaining work. This is often a good strategy when you stand half a chance in your other courses, and investing more time and effort in this course would be throwing good money after bad.

 BEST-KEPT SECRET. Some professors have hidden rules that won't allow you to pass the course without doing all the tests and/or papers; others average in a zero on a hundred-point scale (rather than an 0.0 on a 4.0 point scale) for work not submitted. So before you blow off a piece of work, check with your professor to find out the cost.

5. **The do-over.** A hidden gem in your college's rule book may be the grade-forgiveness policy. This is a policy that allows you to retake a course you failed (or got a very bad grade in) and replace the grade with the one you earned the second time around. Before you decide to go this route, make sure you understand all the fine print in this

rule. Usually, you have to take the exact same course; this can be a bummer if the course is offered only every two years. Also, most colleges only allow you one or two throws at this chance. So don't expect to keep pulling the same trick.

EXTRA POINTER. At some schools the grade-forgiveness program might have a cap on how much forgiveness you get: you might get a maximum of a C replacement grade or the average of the grades. Look before you leap.

6. **The dispute.** If you're up-to-date in the class work but not happy with your grade, you might consider "inquiring about"—or, in street language, disputing—your grade. Normally, this has to be conducted with the professor of the class: going to a higher-up (such as the department chair or the dean) rarely works and really angers your professor like nothing else. (See "10 Surefire Ways to Piss Off Your Professor" on pp. 137–140 for more on this.) You can, however, go over the head of your TA to the professor, since TAs are low enough on the food chain for you to get away with this, and who cares if they get pissed off, anyway?

Grade disputes work best in cases of computational errors, or when a grader has accidentally not read parts of an exam or a paper, or—sometimes—when the comments show that the reader hasn't understood what you meant. Your chances of success are nil, though, when you argue for a better grade simply because you "tried hard" or "just aren't a B student." Whatever your tack, go in person, be polite and respectful, but make your case firmly and straightforwardly. It's a good idea also to offer to leave your work with the professor for his or her review.

5-STAR TIP. In an effort to discourage exactly the activity you're engaged in, some professors reserve the right to lower (as well as raise) grades upon review. You might want to ask—discretely and delicately—whether your prof does this.

7. **The beg.** If your professor is a real softie, he or she may give you a chance to improve your situation through extra-credit work, exempting you from a piece of work, letting you redo a paper or test, allowing you to count some piece of work twice, or giving you some other sort of bonus. Here it really helps to be unbelievably nice and throw yourself upon the mercy of your instructor.

One thing you never want to try is:

The cheat. Cheating is disgusting, filthy, and immoral, and you're only cheating yourself. And what's more, you could get caught. Professors today are very alert to cheating. Many use special software (like WWW.TURNITIN.COM), cruise online paper mills, check student papers one against the other, and know the relevant literature like the backs of their hands. So if you think you're in a hole now, you might find yourself in the Grand Canyon if you get caught cheating. Spare yourself the grief.

10 Signs You're in Real Trouble at College

Some college students are in serious trouble, but don't even recognize it. They think that nothing is really wrong, that everyone else is in the same boat, or that college is just supposed to be hard. Other students are just not sure: "Am I doing bad or really bad?" they wonder. "Should I take some bold action or just wait it out, hoping it'll get better?" To help you decide whether you're in serious difficulty or just caught up in the ordinary ebb and flow of college, here are ten signs that you're in real trouble at college. If you exhibit any of these signs, it's time to do some major reassessment—and make some big changes:

1. **Your grade point is below C or you're getting D's in some of your courses.** Don't kid yourself, C is a bad grade, and D is even worse. A lot of students in college are getting A's and B's (at many schools the average GPA is between B and B+). So if your quizzes and tests are coming back C's and D's, be aware that you are learning very little (and in some cases, virtually nothing) in the courses you're taking. As you move into more upper-level courses, you're likely to find yourself unable to muster up even C's and D's, and instead will be ending up with F's.

2. **You're constantly asking for (and even getting) extensions and incompletes.** Extensions and incompletes are supposed to be the exception, for very special circumstances, not the rule. If you find yourself depending on them as a regular educational crutch—one day the reading took longer than you were expecting, another time you couldn't get enough pages written, a third time you were too busy with your four other courses to bother with this one—you're demonstrating that you aren't able to keep up with the pace of college.

3. **You can't follow what the professor says in lecture—ever.** Most students have moments when they can't understand a point the

professor makes in lecture (see "10 Things to Do When You Can't Keep Up with the Lecture" on pp. 144–147 for things to do in this case). But if all of your lectures are incomprehensible to you, every time, then consider yourself to be in way over your head.

4. **You're spending every waking moment of the day doing the reading or the homework problems.** Professors are well aware of the time constraints placed on students taking five courses a semester and often working part-time, as well as participating in extracurricular activities. So the assignments are geared to be done in a manageable period of time: somewhere between one and three hours per class. But if you're missing by a mile—always—you probably are lacking basic skills expected for the course or are using wholly wrong study strategies (see the "How *Not* to Study Guide" on pp. 55–58 for some of these strategies).

5. **You're living off your credit cards.** If you can't afford your dinners or textbooks without relying on credit, then you are stretched too thin financially. Going to college is a big commitment of both time and money, and trying to get an education at the edge of bankruptcy is likely to put more pressure on you than the average person can manage.

6. **You can't get through the basic requirements.** Some students find themselves unable to pass even the lower-division requirements in math, English composition, and history—and in some cases the developmental (a.k.a. remedial) courses in math and English required before getting to these requirements. Being unable to pass these or needing multiple attempts to pass them is a sign that you aren't academically ready for college.

7. **You're going home every weekend or on the cell phone with your parents five times a day.** Hand-holding and support are one thing, total dependence (or codependence) another. If you're unable to make any break from your parents, you're not ready for the independent living—and thinking—that go with college away from home. Of course, you could go to school in the neighborhood, but it'd be a good idea to take some steps into adulthood some time.

8. **You can't get through the day without self-medication.** We're not talking about prescription medications you might need for a medical problem or chronic condition, but about meds, drugs, or alcohol that you use for recreation or for altering (or balancing) your moods. Most students indulge in some partying at college, but once you get into heavy substance abuse, it's impossible to maintain the discipline and mental focus needed for success at college.

9. **You spend every waking moment on some medium.** It's perfectly fine to interact on Facebook for a bit each day. But when you're texting, tweeting, and tagging without stop—you can't live for fifteen minutes without a device—you leave yourself no time to study (or for much of anything else). If you find yourself unable to get through a day without your computer or cell, consider yourself to have a media addiction that needs to be broken.

10. **You feel overwhelmed—all of the time.** It's normal to feel pretty stressed out at the beginning of each semester and, of course, at midterm and finals times. But if you find yourself struggling every week of the semester—waking up each day hating where you are—something is wrong. Really wrong.

What, Then, to Do? The 7-Step Approach

So maybe you've recognized these symptoms in yourself or in someone you know and love. But what should you do? Here's our seven-step plan:

1. **Pinpoint the problem.** It's easy to feel overwhelmed when you're hit with the perfect storm. Everything's screwed up: your schoolwork, your health, your relationships, your grades. But usually there's one problem that's more serious than the others, and that's spilling over into the others and making them worse. Find the single most acute problem—the one that, if you could change just one, you'd change it—and begin to work on it. This can fix five things at once—especially if the problem you select is at the root of the others.

2. **Figure out if it's soluble.** Not every problem can be solved. And not every problem can be solved in the short term. If you're in serious grade difficulty, you're not going to be able to dig yourself out in one semester. If you're chronically depressed, a few visits to a counselor are not going to make you happy. If you're in major debt, a part-time job will not take care of your whole problem. Still, it's worth making a plan and getting started—since you'll start to feel better as you take a positive step, and even a little progress toward solving a problem is progress.

3. **Make use of campus resources.** Colleges invest a tremendous amount of money in providing academic, financial, psychological, and clinical services to their students. And since colleges often attract the best minds, the professors, advisers, counselors, and clinicians who provide these services are often very gifted individuals. Check out the college Web site, your adviser, or a professor whom you feel you can trust for direction. And if you're at your wit's end and can't bear negotiating the university bureaucracy, call the dean of students and ask for advice: he or she will know what to do. For peer-to-peer counseling, try your dorm counselor or resident adviser.

4. **Talk to a confidant.** If you're ashamed of your problem—or don't want the university to know about it—find a trusted friend, parent, minister, doctor, or lawyer outside the university and talk to him or her. Most professionals are bound by confidentiality laws (if in doubt, ask) and can either offer help themselves or point you to community resources that will work with you to solve your problem. And simply having someone to talk to about what's bothering you might provide some immediate relief.

5. **Enlist a professional.** Certain problems are more serious. Significant legal difficulty, serious health problems, various addictions, or over- whelming debt—these are problems that require extended and pro- fessional treatment. In some cases, you will not be able to solve the problem while remaining a full-time student (or sometimes a student at all). Colleges know about these sorts of problems and are sympa- thetic (after all, they've made an investment in you). So once you've figured out a plan of treatment, go to your college—often the dean of students is the right address—and request a leave of absence. You may be surprised to hear they'll hold your place and in many cases keep your financial aid, too. Much better than to stay enrolled and mess up.

6. **Accept the realities (change is difficult).** If things aren't going well for you, accept the fact. Sometimes you've made mistakes that put you in the position you are in, and sometimes, through no fault of your own, things are going badly. But in many cases change is pos- sible—though difficult. Some problems are habitual—they've been reinforced many times by ill-advised behaviors—and some problems arise swiftly and suddenly. In either case, you should make peace with your situation and realize that the problem won't be solved in a day.

7. **Decide what to do.** Your best shot is to take decisive action. Identify the problem, get help, devise a few alternative remedies, pick one— then do it. You might not be picking the perfect solution—who can, when the situation seems dire? But you will have done something that will, to one degree or another, help you with your problem. Sure beats sitting on your hands and doing nothing.

8

THE SECOND HALF OF COLLEGE

A s you make your way through college, you'll face an increasingly broad array of choices. Many of these center around what to choose as a major and what to do after college. Some more far-sighted, goal-oriented students may have already been thinking about their postcollege life from the very first day they walked onto campus. Others have the "no wine before its time" mentality: they face the choice of majors, and ultimately the choice of career, only when they absolutely, positively, without a doubt must.

But whichever type you are, the second half of college can be a wonderfully exciting time: a time to decide who you really are and what you want to devote (at least the next part of) your life to. Part of the reason it's so exciting is that the stakes are high. When you invest a lot of time and money in pursuing a college degree, you want to be sure what comes out the other end—the real-world end—is a fitting culmination to all you've put in.

The tips in this chapter will help you make the right choices in the later parts of your college career. And the good choices you make in the second half of college can propel you into continued success—long after your days at the big U have become a distant and beautiful memory.

In this chapter you'll learn:

▶ How *Not* to Pick a Major

▶ 13 Skills You'll Need for a Career—and How to Get Them at College

▶ Top 10 Myths About Study Abroad

▶ Transfer Tips—from Community College to 4-Year College

▶ The 10-Step Program for Thinking About Grad School

▶ 10 Tips for Finding a Job

How *Not to Pick a Major*

For many students, picking a major is the single biggest academic decision they'll have to make at college. It's also the one most fraught with mistakes, ranging from picking at the wrong time, to picking without good information, to picking for the wrong reasons. All of which can be easily avoided if you look over—and resolve not to make—the fourteen most common (and most costly) mistakes students make in picking their major:

1. **Picking too early.** Believe it or not, at many schools students are under considerable pressure to declare a major as part of their first-year orientation or at some point in the first year. But it's easy to get stuck on the wrong track. Resist the temptation to declare just because some adviser is pressuring you to do so—or offering you gifts or bribes to decide (like guaranteed places in hard-to-get-into classes, a real professor as your adviser, or quicker time to a degree).

 REALITY CHECK. If there's some good academic reason to declare early—like the music performance major's required five years of practice or the premed program's four years of two-semester sequences—then by all means take the plunge. Just make sure you're reasonably certain you want to study that field.

2. **Picking before you've considered all the options.** At some schools, especially large state universities, there are literally hundreds of majors to choose from (at last glance, UCLA had 346 majors and programs). Don't put your dime down before you've considered a good number of the alternatives. And don't be put off just because you don't quite know what immunology, paleobiology, international development studies, ethnomusicology, or civil engineering are (these five from the UCLA list). Find out. Take a course, or at least stop by the departmental office or Web page and get a description of what they have to offer.

3. **Picking before you've had at least two or three advanced courses in the field.** It's tempting to pick a major just because you liked the subject in high school—or aced an intro or two in that field at college. But it's important to take a sampling of advanced (at some schools called upper-division) courses before committing to that major. The work at that level can be much more challenging, and could differ in approach, methodology, or sophistication from the watered-down version they teach in intro.

4. **Picking something you're not good at.** As surprising as it may seem, there is a regular cadre of students who major in fields they aren't doing well in or don't have the skills for. Rule of thumb:

   Getting lots of A's in a field = good choice of major

   Some A's and some B's = not a bad choice

   All B's = there could be a better choice

   Lots of C's = fuggetaboutit.

5. **Picking something you don't like.** You're going to have to take ten or twelve courses in your major, so it'd be a nice touch if you actually liked the field. Of course, a burning passion for the discipline would be best, but let's face it—only one in ten students has that. (Maybe it's you.)

 EXTRA POINTER. Never pick a major just to please someone else. Just because your parent, older sibling, best friend, or guy you just met at the student union thinks it'd be a bang-up idea to major in something doesn't mean it's right for you.

6. **Picking only because the school is strong in that field.** The fact that the university has a national reputation in nanotechnology won't help you if you don't like small things.

7. **Picking *in spite* of the fact that the school is weak in that field.** Especially in this time of budget squeezes, not every college is strong in every major. And even otherwise good schools can have abysmally bad departments in fields that they don't support or they underfund. Pick something on the upswing, not something dying.

REALITY CHECK. If you find that a school has only one or two faculty members in the area; that very few courses are offered each semester; or that the faculty teaching in that field don't have advanced degrees (hint: look for the PhD after the teacher's name), look at another major. You're likely to be disappointed in this one as the courses roll on.

8. **Picking because you're enthralled by one professor.** Any major is going to require you to study with a broad variety of professors, so don't let some cult professor lure you into a department full of bad teachers or mediocre scholars. You're going to be stuck with this field long after the idol is gone.

9. **Picking because it's easy or has few requirements.** What good is a major in which you learn nothing or that lets you do whatever you want whenever you want? 'Nuff said.

10. **Settling for second (or third) best.** Some students, especially those at small colleges, pick some major simply because the major they'd really like to take isn't offered at their college. If what you want to study isn't on the official list of majors and programs, consider constructing your own major. Many colleges allow the possibility of interdisciplinary or self-directed programs of study.

BEST-KEPT SECRET. If you find there's just no way to make it work given the puny offerings at your school, you might consider consortiums of schools or other colleges in the same city for which your school allows cross-registration (for instance, the Five College Consortium in Amherst, Massachusetts, or the exchange program between Columbia University and either the Juilliard or the Manhattan School of Music). And if all else fails, consider transferring to a college that has what you want. Lack of a major is considered by admissions officers as one of the best reasons for trading your little college for their ginormous university.

11. **Picking only on the basis of career prospects.** Sure, in a tight economy it makes good sense to pick a major with an eye to what jobs you can get, but that shouldn't be the only reason for picking a major. For one thing, there's not always a one-to-one relation between majors and careers. You don't need a degree in marketing or business for a career in the corporate world, or a major in philosophy or political science to have the inside track to law school. Indeed, there is a slew of jobs—perhaps most jobs—for which a particular major is not required, but only skills in math, writing, communication, foreign languages, or analytical thinking, which you can acquire in any number of different majors (for more on this topic, see "13 Skills You'll Need for a Career—and How to Get Them at College" later in this chapter, on pp. 167–169).

 5-STAR TIP. Check out the Web sites of major business publications—for example, the *Wall Street Journal, BusinessWeek, Forbes, U.S. News & World Report, CNN Money, Fortune,* or the *Economist*— for their gurus' best prognostications of what jobs will be hot five years from now. Think disease mapper, robot programmer, information engineer, radiosurgeon, and Second Life lawyer (list courtesy of *CNN Money*).

12. **Picking the *wrong* major for the career you want.** You'd be amazed how often this happens. We've recently seen a student wanting to teach at college level but taking an education degree (intended for elementary school teachers), and a would-be missionary planning to major in anthropology (a field in which proselytizing is an absolute no-no). If you're matching major to careers, make sure to ask an expert in the field—for example, a favorite professor, the undergraduate adviser, or some professional actually practicing the field— which careers go with which majors.

13. **Piling 'em on.** Some college students think it's a special badge of honor to amass as many majors as they can: a double, sometimes a triple major, combined with a minor or two. If a double major makes sense—say, in Chinese language and international relations,

or economics and environmental science, or business and psychology—then by all means go for it. Just keep in mind that each time you add on a major, you're signing on to ten or twelve courses in a field, many of which are required and might not be related to what you want to learn.

 IOHO. There's no cachet in piling on minors, either. It's usually a better idea to pick the four or five courses that interest you, or that support your major, rather than taking the prepackaged minors that many departments offer to attract additional students.

14. **Obsessing every waking hour about which major to pick.** Don't tie yourself into knots thinking that your choice of major is a bigger commitment than it is. Your major does not freeze your future or put you onto a career path from which there is no escape. Department of Labor statistics show that the average U.S. worker changes careers three to five times in his or her lifetime. So relax. Make your best pick and enjoy where life takes you.

13 Skills You'll Need for a Career—and How to Get Them at College

In the new, twenty-first-century economy, students are more worried than ever about what kind of career awaits them. The best way to increase the odds that the job you'll get won't involve waiting tables or flipping burgers is to get the career skills you need while you're still in college. But what are those? Here is a baker's dozen of the most critical job skills that every college student should try to get:

1. **Writing clearly and forcefully.** Students often don't recognize how important writing skills are in many professions. Many students, without a trace of shame, proclaim "I can't write," and consistently avoid courses that require papers. But the "I can't write" excuse won't cut it later on, when you have to write a strategic plan for your business, draft briefs for your legal case, or pitch your advertising plan in a report to the client. Actively seek out college courses that give you lots of opportunities to write. And use the feedback you get on each writing assignment to impel you to improve on the next.

2. **Systematizing and organizing data.** Many jobs require employees to do quite a bit of numbers crunching and to create numerous spreadsheets and tables. Be sure you take courses that teach you the skills to do this kind of work—math, statistics, and the like. Even students in liberal arts majors should come out of college being able to handle a reasonable range of quantitative tasks once they hit the real world.

3. **Doing research.** In this Internet age no one seems to be actually reading books in a library much. But there's more information out there, so being able to conduct research is even more important than before. Courses that include research assignments—usually upper-level classes in the humanities and social sciences—will give you experience with a number of research tools, many of them

electronic, that you can utilize when you come up against research assignments at work. (See our "16 Techniques for Doing Research Like a Professor" on pp. 118–122 for more on e-research.)

4. **Presenting material orally.** In many jobs you'll spend more time than you can possibly imagine attending meetings or giving presentations. Needless to say, when your boss asks you to comment at a meeting or give a presentation, it's not so great to plead shyness or fear of public speaking (as many college students routinely do when asked to present material in class). College offers you many possibilities for training in public speaking. Yes, there's the speech or communications class or going out for the debate team, but smaller classes and seminars often require presentations, too (see our "15 Strategies for Painless Presentations" on pp. 67–70 for some tips).

EXTRA POINTER. Make sure you get proficient in some kind of presentation software, such as PowerPoint, and learn to use all its features, including video and multimedia.

5. **Taking notes.** Maybe you like to sit back in lecture and enjoy the passing show without bothering to take down a single note. Or maybe you write only from time to time as you focus in on what the prof is saying. Not a good idea for college. And even less of a good idea when your boss asks you to remind him or her in detail of what plans for the big campaign were brainstormed in last week's three-day retreat. Every college class gives you an opportunity to become an ace note taker, so don't blow the chance. (See "10 Secrets of Taking Excellent Lecture Notes" on pp. 59–62 for some pointers.)

6. **Reading carefully.** When you get that high-paying job as a financial analyst, you'll have to interpret every word of the minutes of the Federal Reserve Board for clues about what changes they're planning to make to the discount rate. Almost every college course has assigned readings, which you can use to polish your skills at careful reading and interpreting difficult texts. (See "15 Ways to Read Like a Pro" on pp. 63–66 for our best tips.)

7. **Basic computing.** Most jobs today require even entry-level employees to know their way around many programs. And college courses allow many opportunities to become proficient not only in Microsoft Word, but also in (depending on the course) Excel, InDesign, Photoshop, Final Cut Pro, and many other field-specific programs. Take advantage of the free training.

 5-STAR TIP. It'd be a good idea to fully master the program when given the chance, not just learn enough to do the assigned project.

---

8. **Making deadlines.** At college, many professors are softies who will offer extensions, makeups, and incompletes for a wide variety of justified (and often unjustified) reasons. But one of the most common shocks experienced by students once they hit the real world is that most clients and bosses expect them to actually meet their deadlines—no matter what unavoidable (and avoidable) events came up in the meantime. Get in the habit of taking your college deadlines seriously and meeting them without exception.

9. **Working on a team.** Teamwork is often a key factor in job success. What worker is a one-man (or woman) band? Group projects at college and work with study groups can give you valuable experience in working in a common effort with other human beings, even ones you might not like. Doing an internship or participating in a research project with your professors can also give you ways to practice working well with others.

10. **Getting along with a boss.** In college, the professor (or TA) is your boss. Learn to get along with your prof, whether what he or she is saying is what you'd like to hear, or not. Think of each office-hour meeting, each Skype session, or each informal encounter after class as an occasion for practicing your interpersonal skills with a higher-up. Collegiality—that is, getting along with others—is one of the key business skills.

11. **Multitasking and time management.** A college load of four or five courses, each with different sorts of assignments and schedules, is the perfect training ground for developing your skills at doing lots of things at once and balancing the time needed for each. If you hone your abilities for handling the end of the semester—you know, that time when you need to turn in three papers and take five finals— you'll be in a great position to handle the crunch season at work.

12. **Seeing a big project through to its end.** You'll be in a position to easily handle jobs that involve large, complex, long-term projects if you've worked on, and completed, a major term paper, a junior or senior thesis, or a sustained science experiment while you're at college. Sustaining interest and motivation over the long haul is a special skill that lots of students have trouble with. Now's a good time to know thy enemy—at least as regards big projects—and learn how to conquer it.

13. **Creative thinking.** You may not know it, but what really characterizes A-level work at college—and distinguishes it from B-level work— is some creative spark that allows select students to see the issue under consideration in a deeper and more insightful way (for more on this topic, see our "Top 10 Ways of Making the Leap from a B to an A" on p. 117). You can develop your creative skills in almost any course—not just courses in the arts or creative writing (which are also fine ways to stimulate your creativity). Try to always go beyond the most obvious points, striving for deeper levels of meaning and more imaginative ways of expressing them. Creativity shines through at any job interview, and beyond, once you get your once-in-a-life-time job.

Top 10 Myths About Study Abroad

Thinking you might want to study abroad? For some, it'll prove to be one of the most rewarding, life-enhancing experiences of their college careers. For others—well, they'll enjoy the fish and chips. Here are the ten most common misconceptions about study abroad from visiting professor Sara Dumont, Director of Study Abroad, American University. Avoid these and you're guaranteed a bon voyage:

1. **"With the state of the world today, it's just too dangerous."** It's always wise to keep abreast of world events and to avoid study in a region that is currently at war or has a high level of civil unrest. But not surprisingly, study abroad programs usually aren't offered in those regions. Your school's study abroad adviser will be able to help you assess the relative risks of various regions.

 5-STAR TIP. Check online resources especially designed for students studying abroad such as WWW.GLOBALED.US/SAFETI.

2. **"I can't afford to go."** For most students, affording a semester, term, or even a year studying abroad is perfectly doable. If you will earn credit toward your degree for your experience abroad and you receive federal financial aid, then that aid can be applied to your study abroad costs. In addition, many colleges allow their own institutional aid and scholarships to travel with the student.

 EXTRA POINTER. Be wary of those who try to talk you into studying on a summer or January break, claiming that short programs cost less than semester-length programs. While the program price may be lower, financial aid is rarely available for study outside the regular semesters.

3. **"All programs are alike, so I just need to pick my favorite country."**
   There are many different types of study abroad programs designed
   to meet the wants and needs of all kinds of students. Ask yourself,
   *Will I study with foreign students or other Americans? Will I have foreign
   professors or American ones? Will I live in a dorm, in an apartment, or
   with a family?* Let your study abroad office help narrow your choices,
   or talk to a student from your college who has already gone on the
   program.

5-STAR TIP. Some universities abroad have special institutes or
divisions for students coming from other countries (like the U.S.).
This isn't necessarily bad, but you should find out whether you'll
be taking the regular courses with the regular faculty or whether
the school has hired special (sometimes less qualified) teachers
to teach the "imports" (namely, you).

4. **"I don't speak a foreign language, so I can't study abroad."** Don't
   forget that English is the native language of England, Scotland, Wales,
   Ireland, Australia, New Zealand, parts of India, and a host of countries in Africa. And many European and Middle Eastern countries—
   especially the Netherlands, Scandinavia, Israel, and Jordan—are now
   offering a range of courses in English, too. But even if you pick a non-
   English-speaking country, you'll find many universities offering hybrid
   programs: some of your courses will be in the native language (here
   you'll attend lectures, take notes, and take the tests in the language of
   the country), while others will be in good old English.

5. **"I'm not in humanities or social sciences, so I can't get the courses
   to count for my major."** While students majoring in subjects like
   history, political science, and languages tend to have the widest
   range of courses and programs available, students in any major can
   study abroad and stay on track for graduation (provided they choose
   programs and plan carefully). Consult the university Web site, catalogue, or study abroad office to see what's offered in the sciences,
   mathematics, or whatever your major might be.

6. **"It's too late for me to study abroad."** Don't worry if it's late in the fall semester and you haven't done any planning to study abroad for the spring or summer. Normally, you apply for study abroad midway through the semester in advance of the one you want to be away. And even if you miss the application deadline, check with your study abroad adviser, because many programs will still have space and can accept late applicants.

 EXTRA POINTER. Sophomores and juniors aren't the only ones who study abroad—seniors do it, too. Just keep in mind the need to plan, if you need specific courses. And be aware that some countries require students to get visas, so if that process takes a significant amount of time, you won't be able to go to some countries if you are a late applicant.

7. **"I'd like to study abroad so I can become completely fluent in the language."** Get real. Learning a language to the point of fluency is a challenging and lengthy process for most people, and even a year of immersion usually isn't enough to get there. Be realistic about your goals—if you aren't, you will become frustrated and not make the most of your experience.

8. **"I'm going to make lots of local friends and travel as much as I can."** These two expectations are incompatible. If you spend all your free time traveling and away from the place where you're studying, you won't have the needed time in your new temporary home to make new friends. If traveling is what you think is most important, then realize you might end up traveling mostly or exclusively with other Americans.

9. **"I'm paying the same fees as I do at my home university, so I should get the same level of services, extracurricular opportunities, and technology."** NOT! You're in a different country; things will be different. Savor the culture you're visiting—and its distinctive character.

10. **"I'm not going abroad to sit in a classroom or a library."** Sure you are. This is *study* abroad, after all. You'll be getting academic credit toward your degree, so guess what, you'll be expected to do the work—reading, writing papers, showing up for tutorials, and participating in classes. Having experiences (the "fun" part) is great, but collecting experiences without the intellectual underpinnings (that is, without the "study" part) can be a very superficial thing, and study abroad is meant to be profound. At least in the best case.

Transfer Tips—from Community College to 4-Year College

Community colleges are hot—even among those students who go on to get a bachelor's degree at a four-year college. The Regents of the University of California report that 30 percent of UC graduates attended a community college before transferring to the UC. And among all those earning a bachelor's degree in Virginia, a third began at, or supplemented their education with, classes from a Virginia community college. Here are ten tips for making the leap from community college to the big U from visiting professor Glenn DuBois, chancellor of Virginia Community Colleges:

1. **Complete your associate's degree.** National research shows that community college students who finish their degree program go on to complete their baccalaureate at a much higher rate than those who transfer with just a grab bag of credits.

2. **Shop around.** Examine all of the options available to you as a transfer student. Consider both public and private four-year institutions to decide which will be the best fit for you. The four-year institution that you had your heart set on in high school may not ultimately be the best choice for the subject you want to pursue.

3. **Plan ahead.** The earlier you begin to prepare for transfer, the better. Visit your top choices, collect transfer materials, and find out if there are any transfer agreements between where you are and where you want to go. The more information you have, the easier it will be to make a decision.

4. **Know which courses actually transfer.** Make sure you are picking courses that are transferable to colleges and universities. There are Web sites, tools, and advisers at both community colleges and universities to help you choose wisely.

5-STAR TIP. Many states have "articulation agreements"—negotiated documents that make clear what's needed to transfer from one higher education institution to another. The benefit to you as a student is that the agreement takes the guesswork out of the process by telling you in black and white what classes you need to take and what grades you need to make to avoid losing hard-earned credits when you transfer. Many states have Web sites with detailed information about articulation agreements and the process of transferring. Some of the best include:

Virginia: WWW.VAWIZARD.ORG

Arizona: WWW.AZTRANSFER.COM/CCSTUDENT

Texas: WWW.TCCNS.ORG/DEFAULT.ASP

Illinois: WWW.ITRANSFER.ORG

California: WWW.CPEC.CA.GOV/ONLINEDATA/TRANSFERPATHWAY.ASP

5. **Don't be shy.** Meet regularly with advisers at the community college. Keep your adviser informed of your transfer plans, and as transfer approaches, set a time to meet with an adviser at your *target* institution. If you try to navigate this process without the help of advisers, you may not be able to maximize your community college courses.

6. **Choose a major.** Pick your major early, and seek advice about the best courses to take to meet requirements. By choosing your major early, you can take the prerequisites that you need for that program at the university. Well-planned course taking will help you finish your transfer program more efficiently, saving you time and money in the long run.

7. **Get admitted.** Make sure you apply to both the institution and the program you want to attend at that institution. If you get admitted to the university, it often does not mean you are admitted to the specific program you want to study, such as engineering or nursing. The deadlines for the university admissions materials and the program admissions materials may be different. Do your research!

8. **Make them show you the money.** Be sure to fill out the Free Application for Student Aid (FAFSA) at WWW.FAFSA.ED.GOV. Call the university admissions office to see if they have scholarships set aside for transfer students—many institutions do. Make sure you meet all of the deadlines for financial aid. Otherwise you may miss out on assistance that is available to you.

9. **Attend orientation.** You may think you do not need this because you already are a college student. But navigating the university is different. Take advantage of the opportunities the university has created for transfer students. These orientations will help ease the transfer process.

10. **Stay focused.** This one is easy to forget. Whether it's your associate's or bachelor's degree, finishing on time is not easy. But it can be done if you are focused and work hard. Keep your goal in mind, even when you're working in your hardest class, which you don't much like. It will all pay off.

Thinking About Grad School? The 10-Step Program

No one should lunge at graduate school. Getting an advanced degree can take four years in the best case (ten years in the worst) and can costs tens of thousands of dollars if you're not lucky enough to land a fellowship. And no one should begin planning for graduate school in October of their senior year. Putting together a good application—one that can really sell— is the product of a number of years of careful planning and doing the right stuff to get yourself ready for graduate work in your desired field.

What to do? Follow our step-by-step guide to getting ready for the graduate school of your choice:

1. **Don't fixate too early.** There's no point making a decision about whether to go to graduate school until you've finished about half of the courses in your major—especially the upper-division or advanced courses. Only then can you see if you like the field enough to devote yourself full-time to working in it. And if you're good enough in it to make it your profession.

 REALITY CHECK. You ought to be getting mostly A's (or at least more A's than B's) in your major area if you're seriously thinking about graduate school. At many of the better schools, only one in ten applicants gets in, and it's likely that the one won't have had too many B's and C's. (Even at lesser schools, you're typically expected to have all B's or better to stand a fighting chance of getting in.)

2. **Get the tools.** Many graduate programs expect you to have certain skills by the end of your undergraduate career—perhaps the ability

to read in one or more foreign languages, proficiency in statistics, or competence in some particular sciences. Make sure you know what's needed for your field and that you've taken the courses—even if not required for the undergraduate major—that furnish the relevant skills. Otherwise you might have trouble getting into grad school in the first place, or have to play catch-up once you get there.

3. **Don't overload with one professor.** It's tempting to take four or five courses with one prof, especially if you like him or her and are getting good grades in his or her courses. But there's a pitfall: exposure to too few points of view might stifle your development in the field and hamper your ability to get three expert letters of recommendation to apply for graduate school. Cast your net too narrowly and you'll come up short, come application time.

4. **Take the professional-level courses in the department.** Focus on the harder courses and be sure not to skip the junior seminar, senior colloquium, or undergraduate thesis. This is where you can distinguish yourself as a serious player in the field, at least among the undergrads. Just what you need to do to position yourself for grad school.

EXTRA POINTER. Skip the throwaway courses—those courses taught by less rigorous professors or intended for the general university population (and hence too easy to prepare you for grad school). Your undergraduate adviser can steer you away from these, if you only bother to ask.

5. **Try before you buy.** If you can, as a senior take a graduate course (especially if there's one in the subfield in which you are interested). Or do an internship or join a research project with a faculty member in your area of interest. That way you'll get a taste of graduate school or graduate-level projects—all the while building up those relationships that are going to net you those stellar letters of recommendation.

6. **Get at least 600s on your GREs.** Some universities won't even consider you for admittance to the graduate school if your GRE scores are below 600. For top grad schools, 700 is often the floor.

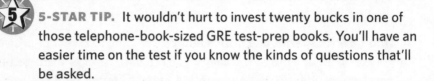

5-STAR TIP. It wouldn't hurt to invest twenty bucks in one of those telephone-book-sized GRE test-prep books. You'll have an easier time on the test if you know the kinds of questions that'll be asked.

7. **Get three bang-up letters of recommendation.** Grad schools pay lots of attention to both what the letters of recommendation say and whom they are from. Good letters come from tenured faculty in the field who have a national reputation, who have given you an A, and who can talk about you and your work in detail. Less good letters are ones written by someone whom no one in the field has ever heard of; from faculty in fields other than your major (unless you're going into a joint graduate program); from TAs (rather than professors); and, worst of all, from family members, your minister, or your Facebook friends (who would read those?).

BEST-KEPT SECRET. Be sure to save all your graded work and give it to the professor when it comes time for letters of recommendation. That way the prof will be able to incorporate specific information about the nature and quality of your work, rather than just writing how nice you are to be around. A more informed—and specific—letter is a better letter.

8. **Give a great sample.** Many graduate schools ask you to provide a writing sample, and the sample can be critical after the first cut in the admissions process. Be sure to submit a strong sample—one that has a topic, methodology, and quality of argumentation and writing that demonstrates your readiness for graduate-level work.

And pay special attention to the suggested length. A school that expects a twenty-page journal-sized article will not be happy to receive your hundred-page senior thesis. (Conversely, a school that's looking for a substantial piece of work won't be bowled over by your four- or six-page short paper.) If in doubt, ask your adviser what's expected.

9. **Write a killer personal statement.** The personal statement you submit should focus on the one or two projects you'd like to pursue once you get into graduate school. Be sure to include evidence that you can actually do the project(s)—that is, that you have the intellectual tools and the background necessary for carrying out what you're proposing (there's no point bluffing or blowing smoke). Your personal statement is meant to be an intellectual plan—not a general autobiography, your musings about the state of the field, or a testimonial about how much you love the field. At least not if you hope to get into graduate school.

 5-STAR TIP. Cognoscenti might want to tailor their applications to particular grad schools (rather than sending the same statement to all). That way, if you've done some work or have some interest that would particularly appeal to some graduate school, you can highlight that in your application.

10. **Don't romanticize grad school.** There's lots of drudge work and many courses to be taken in all aspects of the field you're going to be studying. If you're going to grad school in psychology, for instance, don't assume that every course will be probing the minds of death row inmates or improving your parenting skills. And keep in mind that grad school is a long haul. Four to ten of years of your life could be a big bite if you think that economics might be kinda fun so that you can figure out whether the stock market will be hitting 14,000 again in your lifetime. Make sure grad school is really for you—and you know what it really involves—before you send in that application.

BONUS TIP. Once you've narrowed your choices down to one or two, be sure to visit the graduate schools you're thinking about. While you're there, sit in on a class or two, talk to some of the professors you're thinking of studying with, and, most important, ask lots of questions of the grad students who are already there. They have been where you're going.

10 Tips for Finding a Job

Many students are worried about how they'll finish college. We hope this book has helped them. But some students are even more worried about how they'll find a job after college—especially given the iffy employment outlook for recent college graduates. What is the best way to approach the job market?

When you are actually looking for a job, it is always a "bad" market. The market in the last few years just happens to be a little more so, especially if you happen to be an auto worker or a Big Law associate. But while many people lost their positions during the Great Recession, others have found interesting and rewarding jobs. There is no one magic formula for finding a job, but there are ways to take control of the process and enhance your odds. Here are ten tips for finding a job from visiting professor Susan Schell, director of career services at University of Arkansas Law School:

1. **Know what it takes.** Different fields have different application requirements, and you need to know what those are for the field you are interested in. Do you need a resume, a cover letter, a writing sample, a portfolio, and so on? You also need to know what these materials look like in your field, and which skills and experiences you need to emphasize. A legal resume is different, both in form and content, from a management resume, which in turn is different from a marketing resume. Don't have a clue? Try to arrange an informational interview with a professional in the field to which you aspire and learn what it takes.

2. **Perfect your application materials.** Always have your application materials reviewed by someone who is a better editor than you. After polishing and massaging your resume a hundred times, you are probably too close to see the nits that need to be picked. Have your materials reviewed again whenever you make revisions or add updates. Don't know any good editors? If you are in school, try your career services office.

3. **Activate your network.** Tell everyone you know what type of job you are looking for. There is no sin in looking for employment, so you need to get everyone in your network working for you. While your hair stylist is not a lawyer or a management consultant, he or she may know one. Follow up every lead you are given; you never know who knows the person who can get you the job you want.

 5-STAR TIP. If you have a professor who's worked in industry or in extra-university work in the field you're considering, make sure to invite him or her to use his or her contacts. Often even an informal recommendation from a professor can open doors.

 EXTRA POINTER. If a parent, family friend, older brother or sister, or employer of yours works in the field you want to go into, enlist his or her help, too. You never know who has the contacts that count.

4. **Join a professional organization.** Most occupations, from restaurant managers to engineers, have professional associations. Join one. (Many have student rates.) Attend meetings, go to seminars, and read the materials. Just as an anthropologist would, you should learn the language and customs of your field, the issues of the day, and identify the key players, so that when you land an interview you will "speak the language" like a native.

5. **Be patient and persistent.** Set aside time every week to check for postings, to do research on employers in your field, and to send out a manageable number of applications. It is probably not realistic to try to send out twenty letter-perfect, individually tailored applications in a weekend, so pace yourself. It is better to send five high-quality applications than twenty generic applications. Treat the job search as a marathon, rather than a sprint. When you work on the job search regularly rather than in fits and starts, it is easier to stay focused and control the stress that inevitably accompanies it.

5-STAR TIP. Three of the many Web sites that will help you in your job search are WWW.JOB-HUNT.ORG, WWW.WETFEET.COM, and WWW.CAREERJOURNAL.COM. They provide job search tips, career research information, company profiles, and many other features. Check 'em out.

6. **Don't treat an interview as an interrogation.** If you are fortunate enough to land an interview, treat it as an opportunity to establish a professional relationship with the interviewer. Know the employer and be prepared to ask intelligent questions. Engage with the interviewer, and do not be shy in letting the interviewer know how much you know about the employer and how much you want to work there. Be enthusiastic, not desperate.

BEST-KEPT SECRET. It's always a good idea to do a little Web research on the company before the interview—and, when possible, on the individuals who will be interviewing you. You'll make a much better impression when you know what the company is doing—and how you might fit in. And while you're at it, Google yourself and check out your own Facebook page to see what your interviewer might be learning about you (this will indicate what you'll need to try to explain away).

7. **Practice out loud.** Try to anticipate the types of questions you will be asked, and practice your responses. If you lack experience or feel uncomfortable in interviews, find someone to do a mock interview with. As with other skills, communication skills get better with practice. And while you may think you have a perfect answer in your head, you won't know it until you actually articulate it. In an interview there is the answer you plan to give, the one you do give, and the one you wished you'd given. With practice, those three answers come together.

8. **Be "on" from the start.** In this age of security cameras, you could be recorded from the moment you hit the employer's parking lot. Act like the employer is watching you from the outset. Dress the part. Be friendly and respectful to everyone you meet. Stay focused. Even if you are left cooling your heels in the reception area, do not be tempted to check your phone. If you cannot resist the temptation, leave your phone in the car.

9. **Make that first impression count.** With everyone you meet at the organization—and especially with the interviewer—you want to make your first impression count. Stand up straight. Look the interviewer in the eye. Smile and extend your hand for a firm, but not knuckle-crushing, handshake. (Again, these introductory behaviors can be practiced with your friends and family to polish your behavior and enhance your confidence.)

10. **Be positive.** Stay upbeat throughout the interview. Smile—it will register in your voice. Do not let the interviewer's facial expressions or tone of voice throw you off your game. Do not assume that a particular answer is "wrong" or that you have "blown it." Stay confident. If asked about a perceived negative, do not make excuses or provide elaborate explanations, give it one sentence and move on. Remember that there is no "perfect" candidate; just be the best you can be.

9

THE END—AND THE BEGINNING

And so we come to the end of *The Secrets of College Success.*
Or do we?

Though you probably haven't been counting, if you've read the book straight through from the beginning, you've seen over 600 tips for college success (634, to be exact). But the three most important tips are still to come. The tips that you will write—and do.

Some students have found in this book many tips they can see themselves using. Starting right away. Others have thought up their own tips while reading ours. And still others—well, you're thinking that if only you thought about it for a minute or two, you'd be able to come up with much *better* tips than we have.

Whichever is the case for you, go get a pencil—or if prefer, your iPad, netbook, Blackberry, or device of choice—and answer the following question (100 points, no time limit):

What are the three best tips for college success that you resolve to do—100 percent of the time, without fail, no matter what the situation?

_____

⭐ **5-STAR TIP #1.**

_____
_____
_____
_____
_____

_____

5-STAR TIP #2.

_____

_____

_____

_____

_____

5-STAR TIP #3.

_____

_____

_____

_____

_____

Congratulations! You've just taken the first—and most important—step on your path to college success.

Got a Tip? Join the Community!

Wanna share? Perhaps you're so pleased with your answers that you'd like others in the college community to know about them. Go to WWW.PROFESSORSGUIDE.COM/TIPS and post your tips there.

And why not post something on our wall at WWW.FACEBOOK.COM/ PROFESSORSGUIDE or follow us at WWW.TWITTER.COM/PROFESSORSGUIDE?

Wanna talk? E-mail us at professors@professorsguide.com—a quick answer is assured! And if you want to invite Lynn and Jeremy to come speak at your school, check out WWW.THESECRETSOFCOLLEGESUCCESS.COM. A good time—and lots more great tips—are guaranteed for all.

FLASH! Are you going to a community college or getting your degree online? If so, we have special tips for you! Look for them at WWW.PROFESSORSGUIDE.COM.

Top 10 People We'd Like to Thank

#10. **Kate Bradford.** Our editor. Takes a lot of patience to be an editor. And a little vision, too.

#9. **Arthur Klebanoff.** Our agent and friend (good contract-writer, too).

#8. **Tom Hapgood.** Designed our Web site and keeps all our graphics modern and cool.

#7. **Michael Kohlmeyer-Hyman.** Our business manager and Jeremy's brother. If there's a better guy, we don't know him.

#6. **The *U.S. News & World Report* crew.** Ken Terrell, Sara Clarke, Brian Kelly, and Terrie Clifford. They get out our blog every Wednesday, and had the idea of tips for college.

#5. **All the folks at Wiley in editorial, production, and marketing.** Lesley Iura, Dimi Berkner, Meredith Stanton, Jim Thomson, Jen Wenzel, Nana Twumasi, and Pam Berkman. They've done yeoman's service in getting out this book in record time.

#4. **Jeff Puda for the cover; Maureen Forys, Jon Schleuss, and Corrine Kohlmeyer-Hyman for the layout; and Sue Blanchard for the Professors' Guide™ logo.** How boring would the book be without them?

#3. **Professors David Christensen and Richard Lee for endless infusions of tips (especially when we were running dry).**

#2. **All our past and present students.** You were the beta lab that showed the tips work.

And the number-one person we'd like to thank:

#1. **You!** Without you there'd be no one to tell the secrets to. Bummer.

WEB RESOURCES

The Web is constantly changing. So if you know a Web site that'd be especially useful to college students, please e-mail it to us at: WWW.PROFESSORSGUIDE.COM/WEBRESOURCES. We'll include your suggestions in the next edition of this book.

INDEX

Notes

Notes

Notes

Notes

Notes

Notes